BIG BUSINESS IN LITTLE ROCK

www.BigBusinessInLittleRock.com

Endorsements

"*Big Business in Little Rock* can help everyone working hard to make a difference. Whether you are looking for business ideas or needing that extra boost to keep you motivated. Just pick one story and you will want to go back and read the others."

- Karl Freeman
Principal Broker, Keller Williams Realty
Little Rock, AR

"As a business owner, I find that I learn something new everyday. Reading "*Big Business In Little Rock*" gave me some important and practical ideas that I can use to make my business more successful.

All I have to do is take a few of these ideas and implement them, which ultimately could result in my business becoming a 'Big Business'. Every business owner and entrepreneur will benefit from the valuable experiences shared in the stories contained in the book and I highly recommend it for every businessperson contemplating becoming a 'Big Business'".

- Tom Harris, President
Dent Doctor®, Little Rock, AR

"*Big Business in Little Rock* is a great read for the entrepreneur who needs a positive lift. **This book is long overdue.** It's in the trenches of how real guys are surviving in this economy. A must, quick read."

- "Cadillac Jack" Hendrix
The Phoenix Company

"There isn't anything harder than starting and running a small business. The best way to gain experience without "doing the time" is to learn from those who have already done it. This is a great book to keep handy for those times when you need a little encouragement to keep moving forward."

        - Beth Mason
         Smart Talk Coaching, Consulting & Training

"Big Business in Little Rock is a six-carat gem in the showcase of the American spirit of entrepreneurship!

Six men share their passion for their business, employees, and customers. Passion so deep, that in reading *Big Business in Little Rock*, I felt like I had received a firm, look you in the eye handshake introduction from each one of them.

Big Business in Little Rock should be the calling card of the Chamber of Commerce within the community, the crown jewel of the Economic Development Commission's marketing efforts, a part of every local Realtor's relocation information kit, and a next-read on the list of every business owner."

        - John Moudy
         Foothills Broadcasting, Inc.
         Lake Mary, FL

Table of Contents

Acknowledgements 7

Introduction 8

Roger Best 11
The Back Story 12
Running A Business Without It Running You 18
Living and Working in Little Rock 21
Big Business Starts with a Small Network 24
A Geek Without The Speak 25
Healing Their Hurts 26
Computers, Networks and Working in The Cloud 31
A Huge Security Risk 34
No Time to Wait 37
A Special Offer 39
BizTek in a Nutshell 40
About Roger 43

Jason Everett 46
The Problem Facing Most Americans 47
My Roots 47
Protecting Your Employees 48
Be Their Hero 49
My First Check 50
Close to Home 51
Coverage That Doesn't Cost, It Saves 51
Financially Solid 52
Meeting Sarah 53
A Growing Family 54
Having a Business in Little Rock 54
"Big City" Roots 55
About Jason 57

Mike Davidson 58
The Birth of "The Auto Guy" 59
The Early Years 60
The World's Best Waitress 60
More Than Repairing Cars 62
"Owning" the Call 63
What I Like About Doing Business in Little Rock 66
Why Parkway Automotive? 67
Giving Back to the Community 69
How I Became "The Auto Guy" (the rest of the story) 70
Summing It All Up 71
A Special Offer 71
About Mike 72

J. Ted Lewis 73
The Key to Success 74
The Road to Little Rock 75
Everything but the Groom 76
A Kodak® Moment 78
A New Beginning 79
The World Within Reach 80
The Creative Genius Behind Floral Express 81
Beauty by Design 83
Here Comes The Bride 83
The Royal Treatment 85
All in a Days Work 86
A Special Offer 88

Mike Bennett 89
A Wise Use of Talents 90
A Little Business That Grew 91
Innate Design 92
Good vs. Great 93
Start Here 95
Bamboo Fly Rods to Billion Dollar Businesses 96
A Complete Library at Our Fingertips 97
22 Years in the Making 98
The Benefits of Little Rock 98

Michael DeLon 100
A New Chapter 101
Being Perceived as "The Expert" 103
Winning the Battle 104
Simplifying the Process 106
Getting Started 107
7 SMART Ideas 109
The Key to Market Domination 111
The 3 Stages of Business 112
The Alphabet Maze 116
The Marketing Triad 117
The 1 Question You Must Answer 124
Fulcrum Positioning 126
Brochures, Business Cards & Other Throwaways 127
Putting It All Together 130
What I Like About Little Rock 131
2 Special Offers 133
About Michael 134

Conclusion 135

Contact Us 136

ISBN: 978-0-9883878-2-9

©Copyright 2013   90Day Author   All Rights Reserved

Acknowledgements

We wish to thank those who have made the publishing of this book possible:

The People of Little Rock!

As you read these pages, you'll realize that it's these very people who cause us to stay here. We live and do business in Little Rock because we believe it is a great city filled with wonderful people. Our businesses would not exist if it were not for you.

We'd also like to give our appreciation to our families and team members. You all sacrifice every day to make our businesses operate. Words cannot describe the depth of gratitude and love that we have for each of you.

Finally, to one other. As members of Catalyst we've grown to know each other at a much deeper level. What began as a way to endorse each other has grown to a think tank of sorts where we share our struggles and opportunities and work together to solve them. This book is just one example of what we can accomplish as we continue to work <u>with</u> each other and focus on building a *Big Business in Little Rock*.

Introduction

Sitting around a conference table one afternoon, we were discussing marketing strategies with each other. You'd be amazed at the ideas that are generated when you get a few business owners around a table talking about how to grow business. This is something we do twice a month as part of a group we call Catalyst.

"Big Business" Authors in a Catalyst Meeting

We purposefully work together to support one another's business success.

As we talked, the idea came out that we should write a book. We all chuckled and dreamed of what it might be, and then went on with our meeting. At the next meeting, one of our members came back with a plan to actually make that dream a reality.

Big Business in Little Rock is a snapshot of each of us, and our companies. We wanted to not only tell our story, but also *why* we enjoy living and doing business in Little Rock. This is a great city that doesn't get the attention it deserves. Hopefully, through these pages, you'll not only learn more about us, but be reminded about how good it is to live and work in this "little" city.

We can choose to live anywhere we want. For the six of us, **we choose to live and do business in Little Rock.**

We all can choose where we want to live and do business. So whether we are sitting here in Little Rock, or somewhere else, it's what's inside of us that makes the difference. People want to do business with people they know, like and trust. *That* is the difference! We are here because we want to be in this community. We want to support local business and the community. We want to give back and make Little Rock a better place for everyone.

It's not that Little Rock drew us… we came because of relationships, the environment and the community. And now that we're here, we love it and want to see it grow.

The members of our Catalyst group are working as a team to grow our businesses and the community. That's why we are involved in supporting the schools, The Arkansas Repertory Theatre, and other non-profits that provide education, culture and support to the people of Little Rock. When the community is vibrant and growing, then other people take notice and business thrives. It begins when we support each other and make Little Rock better today than it was yesterday.

For example, Mike Bennett recalls going out of his way to support a locally owned convenience store and gas station because he desired to live in that area in the future. It was out of his way to go there, but Mike wanted this store to still be there selling milk on a Saturday night when he needed it. "I wanted to support Joe….," says Mike.

It's this same attitude that drives us, and many like us, to do business with locally owned companies as much as possible. We all provide valuable service to our customers and we're not the only place someone can buy from. But when we "keep our money at home" by supporting local business owned by people living in this town, we all join together to make Little Rock a better place to live.

We have no plans on leaving. We're serving our customers and some of us are expanding. We believe in this "little" city and are doing what we can to make it better.

Our hope is that you'll join us in our optimism. Whether or not Little Rock is recognized by the media as a great place to live and do business, you and I know that it is. As long as we are able, we intend to invest in local business, the schools, the arts and serving those less fortunate. We believe this is the path to making any city a better place to live and work.

Having a Big Business in Little Rock is more about treating people right and giving back. It's not the revenue we're talking about, but the avenue of investing our lives into the lives of others.

We hope you thoroughly enjoy reading our ramblings. You probably won't see us on the NY Times Best Seller list any time soon, but more important than that, you <u>will</u> see us around town and involved in the community. That's how good cities become great cities – when people get involved.

Thanks for reading *Big Business in Little Rock*. We look forward to hearing your feedback.

Roger Best	Jason Everett
Mike Davidson	J. Ted Lewis
Mike Bennett	Michael DeLon

www.BigBusinessInLittleRock.com

Roger Best

The Back Story

I was 8 years old when I entered the entrepreneurial world. I'm that guy who really doesn't know much other than starting businesses and hopefully, over time, building them up and selling them or doing something with them to serve others. That's about all I've ever done and it happened because my dad asked me to start a fire.

My dad was a pastor. And he took his first full-time pastorate when I was 8. We moved to a small town outside of Kansas City called Lexington, Missouri. That was in another day and time so we did some things that are not "accepted" practices today.

To make a long story short, one day he sent me out to burn trash out back of the house. I had not much more than gotten the fire started when a torrential rain came and put the fire out. I ran inside to keep from getting soaked and waited a couple days, then I was sent back out to start the fire again and finish what the rain had stopped. As soon as I got the fire lit, worms started coming out from beneath this pile of wet trash like I had never seen before. So I quickly grabbed a five-gallon bucket and started scraping them up and throwing them in the bucket. When I had gathered all the worms that tried to flee the fire I went to dad and said, "Dad, either we need to do a lot of fishing or we need to find a place to sell these worms."

We went over to a local bait shop. In that 5-gallon bucket I probably had 5 inches of nothing but worms. It was an unbelievable amount of worms that I had picked up. So I took them all to the bait shop and the bait shop owner said, "I'll give you $5 for those." I agreed, took the five bucks and she asked if I could get more. I figured that if those worms showed up that easily, I would be able to reproduce the conditions that brought them in the first place so I assured her that I could.

She said that if I could get more, she'd give me half-a-penny apiece. I'm pretty sure she got a much better bargain for that first batch but she did have to do the work of separating them into individual containers. I was pleased with the transaction. Our new deal was that I was to gather them and put them in cartons of 50 and deliver them to her as she needed them. She ended up calling about 3 times each week and ordered between 50 – 75 cartons with each order.

So I started raking leaves into piles in the hollow behind the house and watering those down to assure that the worms would be readily available when needed. I'd count them out in little containers of 50 and I'd put a handful of the leaves in the carton to keep them moist and take them over to her. I was 8 years old then, and that was a very long time ago because I'm about two years older than dirt right now. I would sell those to her for a half-a-cent apiece and I was pulling in about 50 to 75 dollars a week in pure profit doing that with this lady. I thought that was pretty cool for an 8-year-old kid.

I went from that to mowing lawns. I picked up my first lawn fairly quickly. It was a 3-acre commercial lot that I started mowing for $7.50. Again, I thought that was pretty cool back in the day. A neighbor saw me with my mower one day and said, "Do you mow lawns?" I said, "Well, I guess I do," looking down at my mower. He asked what I charged and I replied, "What'll you give me?" and he said, "How about $10?" So I looked at his lawn (which was about ½ acre) and he said I could use his riding mower and edging equipment so the deal got even sweeter. So I added his lawn to the mix. Then one day while I was mowing that lawn, the owner of the gas station about half of a block away on the corner walked down to me and said, "Do you mow lawns?" And I looked down at the mower again and said, "I guess I do." (I know, there's a theme that seems to run through this story.) So he said "What'll you charge?" I answered, "What'll you give me?" He said, "How about $15?" So I started mowing his lawn, which was about 100-foot long by 50-foot wide, flat, no trees, nothing, just a lot behind his gas station. Anyway, short version of the story is before I ran out of neighbors I had picked up another $50 to $60 a week mowing lawns by simply being available.

I was really disappointed when dad left that church and we moved to another place because I thought we had a gold mine there. That was the beginning of my entrepreneurial ventures.

I was 14 when we moved away from there and dad again took another church. I was anxious to continue the lifestyle to which I had grown accustomed and anxious to find some way to earn money in this new location, so I started checking around. One of the deacons in the church had a mechanic's shop and Laundromat (I later found out that he owned a LOT of businesses around that small town). When I inquired of him, he said, "I've got a '36 Chevy coupe that I've had for 2 years and have been planning to restore. I've not had time to work on it, so I will pay you to do that work. It's hard, nasty work… are you up to it?" So I began restoring the '36 Chevy Coupe right down to the frame using a steel wire brush, and removing all the rust from the frame. I worked myself up from there – the whole nine yards.

That project kept me busy for a year or two and gave me continuous work and an income even in the wintertime so, once again, I thought that was pretty cool. The day I turned 16 I began working at a supermarket, back in the meat department. I was wrapping meat and cleaning up after the butchers, keeping the cooler cases stocked and all the things that the higher paid staff didn't want to do. About 6 months later I was moved into the grocery department and was quickly promoted to assistant manager. I did that for several months until the end of my junior year of High School. I then left home and went to Springfield, Missouri and finished up 2 credits that I still needed to graduate. I went to class 2 hours a day and then left school for the rest of the day under the COE program—cooperative occupation education—which gives you class credit for working in the open market. I did that until I graduated, then started college and resumed my pattern of figuring out ways to "do my own thing" again.

The first thing I got into was selling cookware. I sold cookware all over Arkansas and Missouri and made some pretty good money, but got tired of all the travel. So I continued my search for a good business opportunity. I went through a number of different businesses during a relatively short period of time. Some worked out well and others not so well. But I found during that process that I quickly grew bored with anything that didn't continually stretch my mind and talents.

During this process I bought a computer. That was back in the time of some really low-end, yet relatively expensive computers like the Texas Instruments TI 99-4A. I bought my first one just before Texas Instruments completely phased that model out of the market so I got a really good deal on it. Like I said, it was a very low-end computer (loosely defined) where the only option they gave you for saving anything you did (programs that I wrote) was to a cassette tape. At that time, cassettes were used for music and to make simple recordings of anything that you might want to listen to at a later time, but Texas Instruments decided it would be a good storage media for programs as well.

I had that computer for a couple of weeks and quickly realized that I had learned all that I could with a device as simple as that, so I moved on to technology that was a bit more powerful. I bought an IBM PC XT, which was top of the line at the time and started looking into all the "things" I could do with that one. I learned during this process that every time I figured out all that was possible with the computer that I had, the technology would change and I had more to learn. Alas, finally, something with which growing bored would be nearly impossible. I began looking into business opportunities in the technology field.

That was back in 1983. You may recall that the courts decided Ma Bell was a monopoly so the Big Bell was broken into a number of Baby Bells. This "birthing" opened up a new market for a company to purchase telephone time from the regional Bell in bulk and resell it to much smaller companies in whatever volume they needed. These types of companies were commonly referred to as "resellers" at that time. If you did it right, the client could save 20% or more on their long-distance charges and the "reseller" could make a really nice profit as well. So I became a reseller.

I had the technical knowledge, but not much money, so I found 4 partners, moved to Little Rock, Arkansas and started a company. Shortly thereafter, I started another one in Texarkana with 2 other partners. Those types of businesses either did really well, or went out of business pretty quickly. Mine were among those that did pretty well. As often happens in a new, up-and-coming business model, the markets grew and a lot of bigger companies started buying up the smaller ones. I had an offer to sell. At the time I thought it was a great opportunity to get some money and move on. So I sold. We moved back to Springfield, Missouri and started an IT consulting company along with a friend. This marked my second stint as a Springfield resident and businessman. I find it interesting to know that Jason Everett, one of the co-authors of this book, was also in Springfield at this time, but it was going to take another move to Little Rock for our paths to cross.

Hindsight is always really good—had I waited another couple of years I would've sold them out for a significantly larger amount of money. But, it wasn't a bad deal, and it gave me an opportunity to move to the next step in business.

Springfield was home for my wife so she was glad to be heading back "home." My IT consulting company grew pretty quickly and I bought out my partner a few months after we started it so I was back in business and ready to roll. I did that for several years and kept trying to grow the company beyond myself. The problem I ran into trying to grow the business wasn't getting more business, but convincing my clients that they were doing business with the company and not with Roger Best.

I'd hire somebody and send them over to do the work, but my clients were always apprehensive that the work hadn't been done properly since I didn't do it myself. I only hired skilled people and they did every bit as good as I could have. My clients weren't so convinced so I would spend all my time running around behind my employees convincing the client that it had been done right and all was as it should be.

Ten or twelve years of that and I decided the only way I was going to grow it was to close it down. I started looking for another company to purchase, similar to mine, but larger. I found a company that was in financial distress that had 7,500 clients... many of which were not the kind of client I wanted but there were enough of them that were within my "ideal client" profile that I decided it would be a good purchase. So I bought the founding owners out of their part of the company and I now had a 50/50 partnership with one of their silent investors. 50/50 partnerships are not a good idea, but that's a whole different story that will just have to wait for another time.

I told all my current clients that I was closing the current company that they were doing business with and that I would love for them to come over to my new company, but that it would be a little different since I'd have a lot of other good folk working with me. Luckily most of them did make the move. The new company allowed me to jump that hurdle of growth that had eluded me for several years. I had 11 employees at the time. Over the next 5 years I grew it to as many as 26 employees. We also expanded from a 3,600 square foot facility to a 16,000 square foot facility.

With just a brief digression back to the story of the 50/50 partnership, I'll say that my silent partner wanted to be more and more involved as we grew and things got better. I knew that I could build an IT company all over again so I began the process of selling my part of the company to my partner. I ended up moving back down to Little Rock shortly afterward and started yet another company. I started as an LLC but decided to Incorporate in 2007 so even though the name changed, I've had this business in Little Rock since early 2001. That's my story of how I ended up in Little Rock. I know, it's long, but it did get me here.

Running A Business Without It Running You

When I purchased this new company in Springfield, it was honestly just a matter of months from bankruptcy. I purchased them by taking over about half of a million dollars worth of debt. I initially thought that if I came in and did all the things that I know to be right about business, things would be fine. I had already looked at the overall picture and had a plan, but I quickly found I was way over my head. I did what I could, made a lot of positive changes and grew the business a bit. The bottom line was looking better, but I wasn't whittling away at the debt the way I wanted. I was working a ton of hours and pushing every button I knew to push, but I just wasn't getting to where I wanted to go.

It was at about that point that I decided to contact some of the many business consultants that had offered their services over the past several months. I talked to a few companies and decided to hire the one that appeared to have the best ideas that would lead me to where I wanted to go. Now I don't know if you've ever had anything to do with that sort of set up. They basically come in and "crawl up your shorts" — in general making your life miserable for about two or three weeks.

They left no stone unturned and I found that nothing was sacred during this process. They had no compunction about telling me all the things I was doing wrong and began to help me build the processes that I needed to move the company forward. Once they had torn down all that I held dear, we began to implement more processes and procedures than I could ever begin to detail here. Finally, they left me with a detailed document describing all that we had decided to be the best plan and left me with the charge to implement. They were available for calls whenever I needed them and they scheduled a return visit every six months to review the progress and make any necessary course modifications. It was a very expensive venture, and even more painful, but the process turned out to be one of the best decisions I've ever made.

I learned that processes and procedures were very important, which up until then was one of my weaknesses. I was just good at what I did and when something came up I would do it. I could train the staff to do the work, in general, but I wasn't doing a great job of teaching them the right process for getting from A to Z without a lot of questions and uncertainty during their trek. I was a "shoot from the hip" kind of guy, and that doesn't make for a repeatable process in a growing organization. Like I said, it was painful, but it taught me a lot about me, the way I lead the company and where that caused a breakdown in workflow and progress.

Over time, through experience and reading more and more books on the topic, I continued to learn how important it was to have well documented processes. I learned that if you document those procedures then the next employee I brought in would have a documented procedure to help direct their daily tasks. It's been a 30+ year leaning process for me, but it's made all the difference in the world.

Today I own a business, but it doesn't own me. I can't say that it all started with those consultants coming in, but they were an integral part of the process that helped to refocus some things and get me heading in the right direction. And I'm not the only guy doing this… I'm not even the only guy doing this that is co-authoring this book; Mike Davidson of Parkway Automotive runs his business in a similar fashion. He has put systems in place to afford him the freedom that comes with owning a business without many of the ties that bind many business owners to their business with little to no freedom. We'd both be happy to talk with you about this if you have interest.

I also learned that it's all about leveraging. There are a lot of different ways to apply that lesson, but we're talking about business here, so let's keep it about business. When I first moved to Little Rock in late 2000 I decided to start another business here and I was fairly committed to the idea that I was going to keep it small and NOT hire any employees. You know, just work it myself. Things took off faster than I anticipated, so I used contract help for a while to fill in the gaps on the work that I couldn't do myself. But I found that contract help often had other priorities than I had and things weren't always done the way I would have preferred, or on the schedule that I wanted. So, once again, I was back in the market to find employees.

Along those lines, there's the issue of **total revenue and trading hours for dollars**. You see, there are only so many hours in the day! I know, that's not necessarily all that profound, but when you look at it from a business standpoint, it has repercussions way beyond simply working and supplying a service to your clients. If it's just me doing the work, I'm tied down to working or not earning any money. There's also the issue of how much money one can make. Leveraging gives you the ability not only to keep things going when you're not around, but it also gives you the ability to remove the income cap. You see, without additional staff, it doesn't matter what you charge, you still only have so many hours to work. So, to make more money you have to increase your rates. At some point, you price yourself out of the market.

But, with a well-trained staff and well-documented processes, you can continue to make a little money off of every employee, so as you grow the business and hire more people, your profits grow as well. And, because of the well-documented processes, your clients receive the same excellent service, regardless of who works on their issues. This makes for a consistent experience for my clients and allows me to not have to spend all of my time looking over the shoulders of my staff to assure things are done right. Simply put, if we really want to get ahead and build something that will last— something sustainable – we must <u>take the time to document and build these processes so we can provide the same great service, every time, consistently</u>. The byproduct of this also gets us out of the trap of trading hours for dollars. All in all, it's a win/win situation.

Living and Working in Little Rock

For me, and the rest of my co-authors, Little Rock is something more than "where we live and work." It's a choice. It's where we've planted ourselves! As you read this book, you'll see a number of different circumstances that brought us to Little Rock. But you'll also begin to see that we thrive here because we've decided that this is a great place to live and be in business.

We don't drive to Dallas to do our shopping; we drive across town and purchase from our friends and neighbors (whether we know those friends or feel that friendship because of the rampant "southern hospitality" that is so prominent here). My wife (Judy) and I live in the River Market in one of the new condos that tower above that part of town. We love our new life there! We have gotten to know our neighbors very well, not only our neighbors that live in the buildings with us, but also the other business owners who have made the River Market their choice for a place to plant their businesses. We can walk into just about any of those businesses and we'll be greeted by name. They know our names because we are there… frequently and repeatedly.

And whether it's the businesses in the River Market, or other areas of town, we choose to frequent the businesses in Little Rock. I find it very nice to walk into my favorite clothing store (Greenhaw's Men's Wear) and be greeted with a big "Hi, Roger" and a firm handshake. I love it when I walk into a restaurant and have multiple servers come by to say hello while we're there and we can chat about what's going on in our lives. Little Rock is an easy place to know and be known, which makes it a great place to be in business.

Like I said, it's a great place to live. If you look at the economy and talk to 10 different people you're going to hear at least 5 different opinions about what the economy is like in Little Rock. But, all in all, Little Rock has a good economy, one that is far less susceptible to the major fluctuations that the rest of the country has been hit with over the past 10 – 15 years. Housing prices have remained far more stable, mainly because they were low in the first place, compared to the rest of the country where homeowners ended up with debt that far exceeded the value of the price of their home when the "housing bubble" burst. During the recent recession Little Rock was far less affected than other parts of the country. Things haven't been perfect, but we've fared much better than a lot of other cities.

There's much to do in Little Rock both from a social and a business standpoint. Socially, we have a couple of theaters that you can go to, and I'm not talking about movies, but theaters that present excellent plays. We love the theater because it's not only a great way to spend an evening, but it's a great place to meet/see other business leaders from the community. We have purchased season passes to the opening night shows at

"The Rep" for a number of years now. We've gotten to know a lot of other people who have helped connect us to other people, which is one of the best ways to grow your business. Little Rock is a pretty easy place to develop relationships. Like I said earlier, we are in the south… you know, friendly people and southern hospitality. Little Rock is big enough to have some things to do but yet it's small enough to maintain a small town attitude – again, it's easy to know and be known.

There's also plenty to do and a lot of great places to eat. Arkansas is a beautiful state with a bounty of outside opportunities… camping, hiking, climbing, fishing, hunting and the list goes on; and much of it within minutes of Little Rock. As far as eating goes, the climate is great so we have plenty of months that are perfect for grilling out on the back patio, if that fits your tastes. Or we have ample options for eating out, many with beautiful outside dining options that let us capitalize on the weather. There's everything from old favorites to a continuing influx of new places and every type of food that you can imagine – I'm starting to get hungry!

Judy and I have lived on golf courses for years, yet we recently sold our home on the golf course and purchased a condo in one of the high rises in downtown Little Rock. Within a few blocks there are 37 places to enjoy an evening out, which is really kind of nice. The building we're in has 99 condos in it. We have a close relationship with at least a dozen of those residents. The building across the street from us has a few more condos than our building. We have a close relationship with at least 30 of those folks. Another neighboring condo building about a block from us is very similar. The short version of it is that within two blocks of us we have a number of people who we consider friends; many more than when we were in Springfield, Missouri, even though we lived in the same neighborhood in Springfield for 14 years. We have gotten to know more people in the last two years living in the River Market of Little Rock than I knew in 14 years living in Springfield.

www.BigBusinessInLittleRock.com

It's not unusual for one of our neighbors to fire out an email or text saying, "We're going for a walk. Meet in front of the River Market tower at 5:00." Or, that someone is having a party and they are inviting the "gang". We may end up with 10 or 20 people going for a 2- or 3-mile walk. It's not only good exercise, but it's always a good time as well. You can name the places in the River Market and there are a number of us there at any given time. So from a social standpoint, Little Rock is just a very easy place to get to know people.

Big Business Starts with a Small Network

Let me jump back to doing business in Little Rock for just a brief minute. The reason I, and many of my co-authors, have mentioned the small-town feel in the city is because that's important to the business environment. As a general rule, a business grows from small beginnings. Meaning, as much as we would love it, almost no one starts a business and is on "easy street" from day one. You have to build it. And that building process happens as we get to know people. Either people who might benefit from the services we offer, or who know people who might benefit from the services we offer. Thus, Big Business Starts with a Small Network.

Getting involved with the community, especially getting involved in things like the Chamber of Commerce and offering to help out with charitable/fund-raising events, will always pay dividends. As you get to know others in the community, they will get to know you and know what you do. My business has been built almost entirely by word-of-mouth and by my involvement in the community (knowing and being known). I know there are a lot of factors to growing a successful business, but if I had to isolate a single key to growing a business, I'd have to bring the "know and be known" aspect to the top of the list. So, like I said, Big Business Starts with a Small Network.

A Geek Without The Speak

One of those things I try to avoid is what's referred to as "Geek-Speak". Every once in a while you run into somebody who is really the techie kind of person and they will want to impress you with what they know. I can speak "geek" with the best of them, so if someone is in that frame of mind, I'm always glad to oblige. But one of the things that I have learned over the years is those techie folk are not my clients.

<u>My clients are the owners and the CEOs of small businesses and they aren't fluent in Geek-Speak</u>. They are intelligent people, many of which are in fields that also share a language that may well be foreign to me, so they could go into a language that would baffle me as well. I look at it like this: when I go into my accountant's office, I know that they have the ability to speak a language that will leave me totally bewildered. But, what I'm looking for is an assurance that they know what they are doing and have my best interest in mind. <u>So I'm always trying to make sure that when I'm speaking to someone, they understand what I'm saying</u>. What my clients are looking for from me is plain English. They want to know that I understand their pain points and that I have a plan to heal that pain. So I work really hard not to go into the Geek-Speak.

I've always been of the opinion that if you can't speak in a fashion that a novice in your field can understand, you only *think* you know your topic. I've always challenged my staff with that same idea. **Speak plain English that our clients can understand. They will be far more impressed than if we try to baffle them with our brilliance.**

My doctor, who I've been going to the entire time I've lived here in Little Rock, has in one of his exam rooms (and I end up in that particular exam room almost every time I go there for some reason) this little figurine of an obviously old country doctor. He's got an old worn-out hat on and a stethoscope around his neck. He has bib overalls on and an old doctor's bag. He has his old work boots on – you get the picture… I'm talking about an old hill country doctor. And the caption underneath the figurine says,

> "You've got the worst case of the
> creeping crud I ever did see."

I love that figurine and I love my Doctor. Partially because I believe he lives by a similar principle of speaking English. Although this little figurine is a bit on the country hick side of the fence, it says something to me about what my Doctor believes. When I go in and talk with him he doesn't throw the medical jargon around. He speaks to me in English. And he speaks to me about personal things in my own life, like where we've been travelling recently or asks me about my car (he knows I love my car). I guess you could say that this particular issue is a big "sticking" point for me. I try to always speak to my clients, prospects, and even people I've just met in a language that helps them know that I understand the world they live in and not just the tech world. There's no reason to go into the Geek-Speak, let's keep the English going.

Healing Their Hurts

Technology is part of business. It's not just something that some folks have/use, it's part of almost any business venture with which you may be involved. I found it interesting that, as I read the other chapters of this book, I found a similar connection and dependency on technology that runs through almost all businesses. I mean, the first thing that comes to mind may not be "technology" when you think about car repair. But, as you'll see when you get to Mike Davidson's

(Parkway Automotive) section of this book, his dependence upon technology is as integral to his business as mine is.

It is because of this heavy dependency on technology that we have as our tagline: "Where business and technology come together." That is more than just a cute little tagline we use, it's something that we try to live by at BizTek Connection.

I read a lot; anywhere from 1,000 and 1,500 pages a week, and have done so for the last 30 plus years now. In my industry if you don't do that you are so far behind the game you will never catch up. Reading 1,000 to 1,500 pages a week doesn't put me on the bleeding edge—probably doesn't even put me on the cutting edge—it just keeps me current enough to speak intelligently about a lot of different topics and keep our clients where they need to be.

That reading isn't solely about technology… it's also about business and interpersonal relationships and what's going on in the world. Why? Because all those things relate back to what is causing the pain or hurt for the businesses in which I offer support. Yes, the lion's share is technology related, but even part of that is more about how technology is used, or should not be used, in the business environment. It's imperative that I stay on top of a wide range of topics so I can have a grasp of the situations that my clients live with every day.

But reading about the latest technology is not something that's unusual in our industry. Actually, it's fairly common. But, unfortunately, what goes along with learning about all this cool new "stuff", be it a program or device, is that we then want to experience those things first-hand. All too often the IT Company uses its clients as the test-bed for those technologies. Or, even worse, they will recommend a new technology because it sounds good, or they just want an opportunity to play with it.

We look at technology as a tool that helps our clients reach their goal. If the new technology doesn't help them be more efficient, open a new revenue stream, or solve a particular pain they are feeling, then we don't push it on our client. I hate it when some of my competition recommends something just because it's available. The biggest problem with that is the focus at that point is no longer on what's best for the client, but how do we make more money with this new piece of technology. That's just not the way we do business.

So, one of the big "hurts" in a great many small businesses these days is related to the business owner having to worry about the recommendations being given by some IT company, or even their in-house IT department. I couldn't begin to tell you the time that I've spent with the business owner just talking with them about the "what" and "why" of technology as it applies to business. It's not a sales pitch, <u>it's about helping them to understand what is good for them, why it's good for them, and how to best implement it within their company.</u>

Whenever I first go into a relationship with a new client, I'm extremely cautious about recommending changes for a while. Without a working knowledge of who they are and what is important to them, recommendations are often based on what's good for the IT Company, rather than what's good for the client. Our son used to wait tables at some fairly nice restaurants. I recall once when he was talking to Judy (his mom and my beautiful bride of 33 plus years, and counting) that features and specials were NOT about what was good for the patron, but what was good for the restaurant. They were really about some deal that they had gotten from one of their vendors… not always because of freshness or value. Judy found that somewhat surprising. She likes to listen to those features/specials and often chooses one for her selection of the evening. But we really like it when we go to have dinner some place and are given honest recommendations as to freshness, flavor or value. It shows that the one waiting on us is willing to risk raising the overall ticket price, in order to make sure that we get exactly what is right for us.

That's why one of my biggest goals is to get to know my client. I want to get to know their business and what's important to them, even their personalities, because personality traits are extremely important in order for any technology implementation to go as planned. We can have the best technology in a client's office and if that client is opposed to certain aspects of it, or even unsure about the what and why, the likelihood it will be a successful implementation is low. Thus, our strong emphasis is on getting to know the client.

When I believe it's time to make a change as it relates to technology with a client, I look at what's going to make that client more efficient, what's going to make them more profitable, and what's going to give them the ability to impact their bottom line. One of my favorite phrases is "healing their hurts." So if we can find something that is causing them pain in their business, then find a way to heal that pain, and explain it to them in a way that makes sense, I'll have a client for life.

Pain comes in a lot of different forms. With many clients it comes in the form of performance and wasted time. I know that many of you have experienced a slow running computer or network! There's never a good time, but it seems that when you need those computers to perform at the best, they tend to do the exact opposite. I'd love to say that this sort of thing "just happens" but, truth be known, it typically happens due to a lack of attention. Oh well, I'll get back to my story.

One prospective client told me about what their typical day looked like as it applies to the technology they use to run their business. His list was long. He told me about how it took his employees between 15 – 30 minutes every morning just to get their computers to the point of being able to work. He also mentioned people jokingly (maybe not so jokingly) going for a smoke (or coffee) break while they waited for their computer to catch up with them. There were a great many other things that he listed, but the point isn't all of his "woes"… it's more about the general "pain" he felt as it applied to his computer/network.

I listened for quite a while before he finally took a break and looked at me with obvious apprehension. He told me about how his current IT company, and others that he had spoken with while searching for a way to heal this particular pain, continually wanted him to simply write a BIG check to solve all of his problems. I began to talk about options, and included ones that could end with him writing a BIG check, but I also presented him with some potential options that came with nominal costs. We talked for a while and he granted me permission to dig deeper into his network so I could speak more definitively, rather than just from an "options" point of view. When all was said and done, he became a client, and has been one for a long time. And within a short period of time, his employees were working when they got to the office, rather than waiting on their computers. They were less frustrated and productivity was significantly improved.

So I guess what makes us different:

> **I don't believe** technology should ever be implemented because it's there.

> **I do believe** technology should be implemented because it serves business objectives; it serves the end goal and it gets the client from where they are to where they want to be.

And a lot of IT companies really don't do that. They look at new technology as a new revenue stream that they can turn their sales people loose on or as something that they're technical people can learn from and play with and, hopefully, get a client to pay for that technology and/or its implementation.

And, all too often, a new technology is not what's needed. It's more probable that the last great thing that someone sold the client simply needs to be implemented correctly and completely. Or it might even be that a few minor tweaks need to be made to get the most out of what the client has. The bottom line is that we won't know what is needed until we sit down and talk with each other. And because Little Rock is what it is, that's pretty easy to do.

Computers, Networks and Working in The Cloud

In business, so long as you have more than one computer, it's pretty much imperative that you have some type of network. Those networks can range from small and quite simple to very large and extremely complicated.

Without getting into a lot of detail, most small businesses have some variety of a technology known as a client/server model, which has been around for several years. We've been in this network environment where we have servers with applications and/or data sitting on them coupled with some variety of client computers. It hasn't been long since those client computers that I just mentioned were either a desktop or notebook computer. Now, they could range from desktops, notebooks, or even an Apple iPad®, Android Tablet®, Windows Surface® Tablet, etc., all needing some type of access to those servers to get to that all-important data.

That's the older method. But, unless you have had your head under a rock for the last couple years, you've also heard about Cloud computing. Now, we in the industry understand that having heard about "The Cloud" has nothing to do with understanding cloud computing! I say that not to slight anyone, but to admit that there are a great many in the IT field that don't completely have their arms wrapped around this subject. There is even a lot of debate within the industry as to what exactly cloud computing is all about. I won't try to tackle all that *is* Cloud Computing, but allow me to at least give you a thumbnail view of what it does.

Cloud Computing simply takes us to the next step from having our employees or staff tied to a location or tied to a particular platform (platform being a program that you're using to access data or even an operating system) that you have to have on your system to be able to access this data. This "Cloud" option now gives us a much more broad-based ability to access data. It also gives us more options on how we work, and how we decide to design and implement networks. Our workforce has a much greater tendency to work from places other than a single office. There may be a need to work as efficiently from home (or even from a coffee shop or the airport) as there is from the office. That may well be possible even under the traditional client/server model, but when you add the BYOD (Bring Your Own Device) tendency that is extremely prominent these days, it simply becomes more complicated and requires a lot more planning.

One of the big concerns I hear is that of "losing control" of data. The data that companies gather and create over the years represents a great investment of time and money. That data has always been what was considered to be safe and secure on these in-house servers, and now someone is trying to get me to move that out on the Internet somewhere. If we do that, all this valuable data will be out there somewhere in "The Cloud" and that scares a lot of business people–especially the smaller businesses. I mean, they are simply trying to keep up with what they do for a living and how to serve their clients best, and now someone is asking them to make a big move to "The Cloud" and they don't have time to sort through all the clutter to learn yet another way of doing things. And so it's not their job, it's not their strong suit, to be able to learn about these new technologies and figure out how to do it or figure out how best to implement them.

So cloud computing is the current "big thing" as opposed to the next big thing. It's not anywhere close to running its course at this point. I believe we will still be seeing new iterations and new functionality out of cloud computing even through the next two to five years. And in our industry predicting anything five years out is a lot like predicting the weather a month away… it's really nothing more than an educated guess.

Cloud computing is here and is growing every day. Even people who don't believe they want to have anything to do with cloud computing are very likely using cloud computing to one degree or another. There are a number of technologies out there, ranging from something as simple as having your email in the cloud, there are things like Google Docs® and SkyDrive®, Dropbox®, Box®, and the list goes on. It's an extremely common thing to have our computers backed up to the cloud, or use things like iCloud® with our Smart Phones.

Products like the more recent Microsoft Office Suite® are built around "The Cloud." I create documents every day that I save to "SkyDrive®" (which is Microsoft's cloud platform). When I do so, all I have to do is to click a couple of buttons and choose "SkyDrive®" to save them there. Then when I try to access them from my Microsoft "Surface®" table PC, it's readily available… it's even easy to access from my Android Smart Phone. And to take that one step further, I can share a single document with someone without granting them access to the rest of the documents that I have saved to "The Cloud" and easily configure whether they can simply read it or edit it.

Cloud computing was not created to confuse anyone or make things more complicated. Quite the opposite, it was designed to give us more flexible options to do what we need to do. *That* is cloud computing.

The diversity of our technology these days makes it great for the user, yet most challenging for the IT support team and business owner. You have your Windows® server that you have sitting somewhere, and there is typically a lot of data housed there, along with a bunch of applications running on them. You might also have some variety of Linux®, Unix® or AIX®, although the lion's share, as it applies to small business, will be Windows® servers. In recent years we have seen things like Google Chrome®, and Chromebooks®, which actually have a web browser rather than a standard Operation System. These devices, and others like them, are designed to access data that's stored in the cloud, allowing you to use a web browser rather than some installed application. They actually do much more than just web browsing or playing around on Facebook® or LinkedIn®. In fact, the Microsoft Word® document that I mentioned sharing earlier comes complete with the ability to edit in a web version of Microsoft Word®, so there is no need for the one that I shared the document with to even have Word® installed on their system. They could, in fact, be using one of the Chromebook® devices that I just referenced.

A Huge Security Risk

You also have your Apple® products like the iPad® and now we have the iPad Mini® which is running Apple®'s operating system, not Windows® in any way shape or form. Regardless of what Apple® and Microsoft® would like you to believe, they do not play well together. Again, none of these things are insurmountable, but they do add a level of complexity for the IT support staff. And securing these BYOD devices is among the most important.

This BYOD initiative is something that affects almost every small business. Almost everybody has smartphones that they bring to work. More and more people have tablet computers like the Android® Tablet or the Apple iPad® or a Microsoft Windows Surface®. All of these represent very different platforms. They also represent the ability for employees to work when they are away from the office. But, most importantly, they can represent a huge security risk. Whether these employees are simply accessing company email or going deeper into other important, and often confidential, company data, it's important that access to that data be safe and secure.

This BYOD culture presents a huge security risk in that those employees own those devices and they take those devices home at the end of the day. They may take them to the airport or a coffee shop, all the while accessing proprietary company data. It's also possible to save that data down to those devices and access them completely off-line. At first blush, as an employer, I like getting more work out of my staff, but it can also be somewhat scary to think about the possibility of that employee having my valuable data roaming around on these devices…which can easily be lost or stolen.

A lot of my clients block sites like Facebook® and Twitter®, not just because of the potential of the employee wasting company time but, even more importantly, because of the risk of the tons of options for infecting computers while on those sites. That risk extends even to those devices brought into the office by the employee. There is a variety of Malware known as a Worm, which can propagate without any human intervention. In other words, if one of those employee-owned devices gets one of those worms, and it's even using the Wi-Fi (Wireless network at the office), that worm can easily spread to other devices on the network.

And so it becomes our job as their trusted IT advisor to be able to implement a strategy to protect the business, help the company develop a policy, and implement the appropriate procedures to help assure that company data, and company networks, remain safe and secure. We even have to deal with issues about what happens if an employee is suddenly no longer with the company. How do we make sure the data is not on their personal devices – on their smartphones, their tablets, whatever the case may be? And what if they leave it at the airport or a coffee shop, or it is stolen from their car? There is data that is now accessible on those devices. Technology today gives us the ability to secure those devices. But remember, the devices are not yours so there needs to be policies in place that implement a protection plan.

I think this is a question that's on everybody's mind: **How does an average business owner get his head around all of this**—or any of it and then wade through it all when there's probably a dozen companies who are all saying similar yet different things? It can be quite baffling to most small business owners. That's why part of what BizTek does is to provide not just the technology solution, but the counsel that the business owner needs so they can better understand all that's going on and how they can best protect their data and their business.

This goes back to one of the things on which I focus from the start... getting to know the client, knowing what's important for them and how critical and sensitive their data is. We understand that all data is important, but not all data is extremely sensitive. Making these decisions starts with a thorough look at the data to evaluate access rules, followed by creating a policy for how much security is needed. Certain platforms allow us to manage these various devices remotely. So if you're out and your tablet, Smartphone or other mobile device is stolen, you're just a phone call away from a complete wipe of all data on that device. We try to give our client the information they need to make an informed decision.

So, for the average business owner to be able to make those informed decisions, there has to be regular dialogues with your IT provider. Whether you have an in-house IT staff or whether you are strictly outsourced through companies like BizTek where we take care of all the IT support for you, you need to have those regular conversations and have a plan. If something changes in the way you do business, the IT support staff shouldn't find out after the fact. They need to be involved in those on the front end so all of the caveats associated with the possibilities have been explored, before you pull the trigger. Trust me; it could save tens of thousands of dollars, even in the short term.

No Time to Wait

We've all heard it said that choosing to not make a decision is still a decision. This, in effect, is deciding to do nothing. <u>Indecision can be one of the most costly choices you will ever make</u>.

I've been in the Little Rock market for years, and over the years I have seen this proven over and over again. For example, there used to be a local division of a fairly large company that we did some work for. The local branch used my company to supplement its own internal IT staff. One of the things that I continually tried to get them to let us handle for them was patching and updating their computers and servers. That's a fairly mundane task and they continued to reject my offers to handle that for them saying that they would do it themselves. The problem was they never did. It was just one of those things that they kept putting off until tomorrow. This was several years ago, and I don't recall the exact exploit (a particular variety of malware that was released to capitalize on a vulnerability in the Windows® Platform) but it was a particularly nasty one. Their company fell victim to the attack and it crashed all of their servers and most of their desktop computers. The sad thing was that this particular vulnerability was one that, had their systems been properly patched, would have had zero effect on them.

Every client that I had at that point in time that had allowed us to take care of their patches for them or did their patches on their own were in good shape. Every one of them came out of that particular attack completely unscathed because Microsoft®, and most platforms out there, are very aggressive at listening to what's going on in the market and who's trying to hack them and who's trying to exploit the potential holes in their platforms. This was one of those gotchas that Microsoft® knew about and had already been remedied via simple patch management. The end results of this failure to make a decision and follow-through with it ended up costing them in excess of $10,000.00 in direct costs and much more in indirect costs. So some decisions aren't good to put off.

The small business owner is frequently just trying to figure out how to keep their heads above water and, hopefully, get ahead of the game in an ever-changing market. The simple truth is that there are very few places that you can get by with doing the same thing (or the same way) you did 10 years ago. If you are, you're likely losing ground at a rapid pace. Business owners have a lot to keep up with on their own.

That's the reason it's so important to partner with a company, like BizTek Connection, in order to relieve yourselves of the pressure of *also* having to be an expert in the technology that your business has become so dependent upon. I mean, being excellent at what you do (be that accounting, or dentistry, printing or whatever) is a tough enough job without adding one more area where you have to become an expert. And this is just not an area that is worth the risks associated with not making a decision or not making the right decision. So you're either putting yourself at risk by not being protected or you're simply falling behind because you're doing things the way you were 10 years ago and now a minor change could take you out overnight. That's why there's no time to wait.

A Special Offer

To help business owners find some peace in all of this, one of the things we do on an as-available basis is offer a **Free Network Assessment**.

This is a 27-point network assessment where we come in and do the legwork to figure out what's going on in your network. We install software that monitors what's right and what's wrong on your network and within the computers and servers. We check everything from a best practice standpoint and look at industry norms for performance and acceptable thresholds to make sure you are getting the best out of the technology that you use within your business. We evaluate any security risks internal to the system that would literally take weeks to find if we were trying to do this manually. And we'll give you a printed report showing you exactly where you are at that point in time. It'll show where your risks are, where you are vulnerable, where you are in good shape, and how well your systems are patched and protected. This process even gives you a complete asset list of all your devices attached to the network, which your finance department will love. It's almost like a CAT Scan® on your network systems. And we can offer that FREE on an as-available basis to anybody that wants this performed.

There's no obligation to it. We've done it for people that have an IT provider or for others who have an internal IT staff. And there's no obligation at the end to start doing business with us in any format. We simply give you the report and we walk you through it and talk with you about what we do and how we can help you. And if it works out for both parties, we will be glad to offer you whatever support you may need. We frequently pick up new clients during this process. But there are times when the company will just take that report back to their current IT provider and allow them to take care of anything that needs attention. Either way is fine with us. It's about building relationships and making ourselves available should the need arise.

BizTek in a Nutshell

Our primary line of business is a category that's known in the industry as Managed Services. Getting that out of Geek-Speak and into English… **we proactively monitor** what's going on inside of our client's computers, on their servers, on their intermediate devices like routers, gateways and even network printers. We monitor what's going on with those devices and do everything possible to keep those systems performing the way they were intended. We have predetermined limits and boundaries that are norms within the industry. Monitoring for these things frequently alerts us to potential issues BEFORE they create a "down" situation for our clients.

You see, when you buy a brand new hard drive (or any piece of equipment for that matter) the question is not *if* it is going to fail… the question is when is it going to fail? It will fail. We watch for signs that the user who is using the system every day cannot see. These signs indicate a potential failure is coming sooner rather than later. We always watch for things that could cause a critical system to become unavailable or cause data loss and preemptively address those issues whenever possible.

Our system alerts us to things like a hard drive that is getting close to failure. We will do things like create an image of that hard drive and replace it before it crashes. This can literally change what could have been a loss of data and days of downtime into a simple matter of taking a system out of production for a matter of an hour or two with zero loss of data. And we can do it during "off" times in order to reduce the negative impact to the business.

Things are going to fail. But in many cases there are some indicators that will alert us to the potential problem. We watch for those indicators in an attempt to avoid, or at least mitigate, the risks. Almost anybody can fix a problem once it's broken, but not everybody can do an effective job at monitoring what's happening on a system to keep them from going down.

Your car has an onboard diagnostic system that monitors most everything and alerts you if there is a problem. That is what is happening when one of the little lights begins to shine on the dash. Unfortunately computers, servers and network devices don't have that same ability to alert you to issues. Our monitors do. The technology used in your business is very likely the very lifeblood of your business. It's our job is to protect it and make sure it's up and running when you need it so you can focus on running your business and providing great service to your clients/customers.

Technology is part of your business. BizTek Connection is "Where Business and Technology Come Together."

I hope that we can "come together" and serve you with our FREE Network Assessment, or perhaps in some other way. Maybe we'll just grab a bite to eat and begin building a relationship. Whatever it may be, I look forward to helping you and investing back into your life and that of this great community. And as we come together, I hope that we'll be able to assist each other in creating opportunities that can benefit this community as we strive to stimulate even more Big Business in Little Rock.

Special Offer to Readers of Big Business in Little Rock

Free Network Assessment

Available on an as-available basis. Call to schedule your Assessment Today.
1-866-851-5321

www.BizTekConnection.com

Roger Best Vcard

About Roger

Yep, that really is my family and me. And, yes, that's really a picture taken in our neighborhood.

We've lived in the Little Rock area since late 2000 but it wasn't until the past couple of years that we actually moved into the heart of the city. We live in a high-rise condo in the River Market, which we've found to be an absolutely remarkable place to live. Our son (at the time of this publishing) is a Sergeant in the Marine Corps, and he and his beautiful wife (who is just as much our daughter as our natural born children) are about to give birth to our first granddaughter. And my baby girl, 21 years old, just completed her third year of college at UCA. Oh, let's not forget my gorgeous wife of more than 33 years. Together, we make up the "Best" family, and our family comprises the best of all that I've ever accomplished.

I've always been entrepreneurial, working almost exclusively for myself since I was 20 years old. As you might anticipate, there were a number of "lean" years in the growing process and my wife's support and encouragement have never (well, almost never) faltered and have been critical to my success. Of all that I have, she is the greatest contributor!

It's only because of the support of my family, my wife in particular, that I've been able to build the successful IT company we have today. I attended Central Bible College, but I know what I know about IT because of my passion for learning how things work and what makes them tick. As a kid I loved to find things that didn't work so I could restore them to their original working state. I got into the IT field simply by someone asking me if I could do a particular task. My answer was yes, at which point I sat down and figured out how to do whatever it was they had requested. That led to another, and another, and another, until I finally reached the point at which I've traveled the country as a SME (Subject Matter Expert) for a number of the latest technologies and represented some very well-known companies in US business.

But I've learned over the years that a lot of people with a passion for technology often don't have that same passion for the business' bottom line. As a business owner and not an employee, I understand that a good bottom line is essential to business success. Almost every IT company is owned by someone who has those same responsibilities, but many of the owners have only held that one position, while others hire someone to lead their company who is just an employee and not sitting at the desk where the buck actually stops. That gives me a unique perspective with my client's bottom line in mind.

We have spent years to develop the systems and processes to help assure that our clients are using technology that is available when they need it. We even put our money where our mouth is, so to speak. Waiting for something to break, calling the "IT Guy" and praying that he gets everything fixed relatively quickly is simply not a good plan for the bottom line. It's a great plan for the "IT Guy" because with each passing minute his hourly charges grow, while the client is losing money due to loss of productivity and those hourly charges. We shoulder the responsibility for these risks by offering an easily budgeted retainer that puts the responsibility to get things working and keep them working on our shoulders. It's amazing how healthy your IT systems become when the technology service provider has to pay to fix any problems. It now becomes our responsibility to mitigate issues before they become a problem, or we pay the bill.

In case you are interested in the "rest of the story" (as Paul Harvey would have said), I love to travel, just about anywhere, anytime. Cruising is a lot of fun, just as much as relaxing on a resort beach, watching the waves return to the sand. I love to scuba dive, but flying above the treetops on a zipline is a remarkable way to spend the afternoon, as well. These, and just about anything that life may bring my way, are what makes my life interesting, so long as my bride is by my side.

Jason Everett

Liberty National
Life Insurance Company
Since 1900

The Problem Facing Most Americans

The day when workers retire, change jobs, get fired or otherwise find themselves no longer employed, is the same day they lose their life insurance coverage.

So the question to ask yourself as a business owner is:

> "Do you think your employees plan on dying before or after they retire?"

<u>The answer is</u>: They plan on dying *after* they retire. That means they need life insurance coverage that will continue long after they leave their place of employment.

My Roots

The start of my career came in the normal fashion. I went to Bible College in Springfield, Missouri and upon completion started working for the phone company [MCI WorldCom]. Of course we all know what happened with WorldCom and Enron during the financial crisis of the 2000s. About this time I bought a life insurance policy and a cancer policy from United American Insurance Company to protect my family and me. Who would have thought that policy would be a turning point in my career?

Shortly after that time, I talked with my agent and he told me about a career opportunity with the insurance company that he thought I'd be good at it. I said, **"NO WAY! I'm not an insurance guy."** He replied, "Well, you need to come and talk with my boss." A few days later, as I was on my way to play golf, he called me and said, "Hey, you need to come by our office right now. My manager wants to meet with you." I said, "I'm wearing golf sandals and shorts." He told me that didn't matter. So I stopped by their office and met with the Branch Manager and realized in that meeting that this was right in line with what I went to school for—it's a way to help people and a way to protect them. It lined up better than a 3-foot putt.

In 2003 I started with the Branch Office divisions of Torchmark Corporation affiliates, United American Insurance Company, and later with Liberty National Life Insurance Company. I was still in Springfield, Missouri at that time and soon realized that – WOW!—this is good! It's good for my family, because I'm able to make a great living; it's good for my clients, because I'm able to help people; and so it was a good fit for my skills and passions.

In 2006, they gave me an opportunity to move back to my home state of Arkansas—Northwest Arkansas to be precise. I'm a HUGE Razorback fan so this was like a dream come true! I stayed in NW Arkansas from December of 2006 until September of 2009. We then opened a Little Rock office because we wanted to be more centrally located since we did a lot of work with county governments. The best place to be for that was Little Rock. It's also good for recruiting new agents because we're able to recruit agents that are more centrally located so we can provide coverage and protection for the entire state more easily.

Protecting Your Employees

Employees are the greatest assets a business has. And protecting your employees is a meaningful action for the business owner and it's really not a waste of time or money.

Too often when we talk to a business owner, they think this is going to cost them money and have no benefit to the company. They think, "My people don't need any more insurance," or "My people don't want any more insurance." The funny thing is, if I was to walk into a room with 50 people and I asked, "Does anybody in here want any insurance?" The answer would be "No."

But what we have found is when we're able to meet with people one-on-one, we find out that they have a need because most people don't realize the fact that on their last day of working they lose their life insurance.

Be Their Hero

The other day I received a phone call from a family up in the northern part of the state and they had a family member who had passed away.

He had been camping in a van and had a heater hooked up to keep warm. He had the door cracked, but at some point during the night had died due to carbon monoxide poisoning. The family had no idea that he had life insurance. He was not one to really think about things of that nature nor would he have bought life insurance on his own. But he worked for an owner who was a hero. This business owner made life insurance available to his employees and this gentleman had $85,000 worth of insurance that was there to take care of final expenses and also to give his three children something to remember him by. It's not a ton of insurance, but $85,000 goes a lot farther than nothing.

We had another gentleman who was a policeman in a small town in Arkansas and who had just purchased a Liberty

National policy. He was healthy and young; or so we thought. He passed away from a heart attack before he had the first payroll deduction pulled out of his paycheck. <u>Had never paid a penny for the policy</u>, but because our policy began the moment he applied for it, he had $25,000 worth of insurance that he wouldn't have had if it weren't for Liberty National. And he never paid a penny for it. How grateful do you think his family was for his decision and that of his employer?

My First Check

I'll never forget the first check that I delivered to a family. I was serving a company in Texas and had just finished enrolling every employee, or so I thought. As I was heading to my car to go home, I noticed a gentleman getting out of a company vehicle and into his own. I ran over and introduced myself and he told me that he was a repairman. I told him that I was there visiting with all the employees and I needed to see him for a minute. So he and I went back inside. We sat down and started talking about life insurance and he said, "Well, I just bought that pickup truck out there and I guess before I die I need enough life insurance so my old lady won't have to pay for my pickup truck." So I asked him how much insurance he had and realized he needed an extra $15,000 worth of life insurance. And within a matter of about 45 days I received a phone call one night while I was at dinner with my family that this gentleman had passed away from an aneurysm.

I met with his wife at a restaurant in Texas and gave her the check and said, "I want to tell you the story of how I met your husband." After relating the story to her I was able to say, "Here, ma'am, is a check. Go pay off the pickup truck."

Close to Home

The reason life insurance is so important to me is that my family has fallen victim to not having life insurance. My grandmother thought that she had paid for life insurance much of her life to make sure that she had enough to protect her family when that time came. Since I was the insurance guy in the family, when she passed away I went in and started going through all of her policies and records and realized she didn't have life insurance. What she did have was just plain accidental death insurance, which she had been paying on for many years. That didn't do us any good at all.

How many people in America are only covered by an accidental death insurance policy that won't pay if you die of natural causes? Or the only life insurance they have is through their employer that ends the day that they stop working? This is where many Americans are – **they are under protected and don't even know it.** That's why I love working for Liberty National and helping business owners become a Hero to their employees.

Coverage That Doesn't Cost, It Saves

A business owner basically saves around 10% of every dollar that their employees invest in insurance. So for instance, if I were to spend $100 per month for my insurance as an employee, that would save my employer approximately $10/month.

> *Times Are Tough.*
> *Being A Good Employer Isn't.*
>
> | EMPLOYEES | | EMPLOYERS |
> |---|---|---|
> | $3,000 Accidental Death Policy | = | NO CHARGE |
>
> ### Jason Everett
> ### 501-225-5556

So $10/month times 30 employees equals $3,000 dollars, and 10% of that would be $300 a month. That's $3,600 a year… $36,000 every 10 years. Not a lot, but every dollar adds up.

The question you have to ask is:

> Is sending money to the government worth more than providing an opportunity for your employees to protect their families?

What better way to express your appreciation for a valued employee when they leave your employment than to thank them for being a great employee and understand that the insurance policy they purchased to cover their family goes with them and that you have made it possible for them to protect their family upon their death. What a great way to position yourself and to help your business gain even more employees as well. It's a simple way for a business owner to be a Hero to their employees.

Financially Solid

Liberty National is rated A+ (Superior) for Financial Strength by A.M. Best (as of 6/12). We're part of the WARD's Top 50 of all insurance companies (as of 7/12). Liberty National is a subsidiary of Torchmark Corporation, a Fortune 1,000 company (TMK on the NYSE). And so we're a major insurance company with solid financial backing.

But yet we have roots right here in the community. We have folks right here who care about your employees. We'll be some of the first out to help the family when a situation arises. We'll be here to help out with claims or just to care for them.

You can buy insurance online, but who's your family going to call if you pass away? You can even purchase cancer insurance online, but where are you going to go when you have a claim? We're right here in town. We're going to be here to help you file those claims and walk with you through the entire process. We're going to be here to help your family make sure that everything is done exactly the way it is supposed to be done. We'll make certain you get every benefit you are entitled to, and we'll do it in a very caring manner.

Meeting Sarah

Sarah and I met while I was attending Baptist Bible College in Springfield, Missouri. Like Roger Best (a co-author of this book) I also realized that finding a wife in Missouri is a *very* good move.

Before Bible College I grew up in Greenbrier, Arkansas. That was neat because I knew everybody who lived there. Of course it's just north of Pickles Gap and east of Toad Suck. So everybody knows where Greenbrier is.

Scan this for a video about Jason

Part of growing up there was spending time with my neighbors, fishing, hunting, spending the weekends together with my dad, and doing things that boys like to do. I had all my family within five miles of me. When I was growing up, we didn't have to use the area code, or even the prefix, all we had to do was dial the number and hope that nobody was on the party line to listen in.

www.BigBusinessInLittleRock.com 53

A Growing Family

After marriage Sarah and I tried for six years to have kids. We then determined that we should look into infertility treatments, so we visited with a doctor in St. Louis. Shortly after that meeting I started myself on the prescribed injections. I then received a call from a friend of mine in Ohio who knew of a young girl in his church who had gotten pregnant and wanted to give the baby up for adoption. We pursued that route as well. With only about three months to go before the adoption was to be complete, the mom backed out. So I knew at this point that it was God's way of saying, "Not now, my son."

About 54 weeks after that baby was supposed to be born, we were living in Northwest Arkansas and our <u>first son,</u> Joshua, was born. We thought he was our miracle child—one in a million. And just fifteen months later we had <u>another son</u>, Caleb. The next year we had our <u>third son</u>, Hudson. And a little over a year after that, we had our <u>fourth son</u>, Titus. And as I'm recording this chapter, we are pregnant with our <u>fifth son</u>, Silas. So this will be five children ages five and under! God has truly found a way to bless us with children, and to Him we are truly grateful.

Having a Business in Little Rock

The great thing about running a business in Little Rock is meeting people. This is a great city filled with the type of people you just like to hang out with. That could be grabbing a cup of coffee at a local diner, taking in a play at "The Rep", or going to a Razorback football game. It's all about building relationships that will last a lifetime. I also love building my business in Little Rock because I have the opportunity to watch the agents we hire come in and build a business for themselves. This really is the American Dream for many people. What a joy it is to be able to help good people find a great opportunity in one of the biggest "little" cities in America.

I've met with a lot of business owners in my career. And in those meetings, I find that we have a struggle in America finding good people to run for political office. I hope one day that I'll be able to help change America's direction toward the right direction and run for office. There's no doubt about it; when you give business owners the ability to grow their business by having fewer restrictions and lower taxes, they'll retain more of their money. This will allow them to expand their business (and our economy) while having more people working. The result will be a stronger economy as we keep more business right here in our state, and that's what we need.

"Big City" Roots

When I was a kid, Little Rock was the "big city." We would come here to see my grandmother who lived in North Little Rock. I remember what it was like as a kid crossing the river bridge thinking, "<u>This</u> is the big city."

What a joy it has been to come back to a town like Little Rock in a state that I love so much and be able to watch the Travelers baseball team play, go down to Verizon Arena to see the different venues, take a walk with my family along the Arkansas River or maybe a stroll across the Big Dam Bridge. I *love* this town!

I enjoy going to church at the Bible Church of Little Rock and being around people that I care about there and throughout Little Rock. This is a community that is very tight-knit. It's big, yet seems so small.

It's good to know that I'm in a business that regardless if I meet you at Wal-Mart or I see you at church, I can look you square in the eyes and know that our policies are going to do exactly what we say they're going to do.

I guess that's one reason I love working for Liberty National. And it's a reason that I'm always looking to hire agents in the Central Arkansas area. I look for people who want to make a difference in the lives of others by providing them with portable life insurance coverage to protect their family. If you know anyone seeking an opportunity of a lifetime, have them check out our website at www.LibertyNational.com.

And if you own a business and want to be a hero to your employees, I'd love to sit with you at a local restaurant and talk about how we can help you and your most valuable asset. Please call my office in Little Rock so we can find a time to chat: 501-225-5556.

From my earliest memories, Little Rock has always been the "big city" for this little boy from Greenbrier. It feels like a dream come true for me to have the privilege of serving the citizens of this wonderful city and state and to be involved in the community as I give back from what I've been given. I hope you feel the same way.

I look forward to meeting you and serving together to make your business a *Big Business in Little Rock*.

About Jason

Jason Everett is originally from Greenbrier Arkansas. He moved to Springfield, Missouri, to attend Baptist Bible College where he earned his degree in Pastoral Ministries.

Jason also met his wife Sarah while attending college and they were married in 2001. Jason started his insurance career with Torchmark Corp., the parent Company to Liberty National, in 2003. Jason and Sarah relocated to Little Rock in September 2009 and have been blessed with 4 boys: Joshua, Caleb, Hudson, and Titus. And Sarah is pregnant with son #5 who is due in August 2013.

Help protect your children with a FREE Child Safe Kit from Jason Everett and Liberty National Insurance.

FREE
CHILD SAFE KIT
Protect your children today!

Jason Everett   501-225-5556

www.BigBusinessInLittleRock.com

Mike Davidson

The Birth of "The Auto Guy"

The year was 1969. I was about five years old and I really loved my mom and I wanted to help her out. I distinctly remember sitting in the car one day and watching a man take a hose and put it in this hole in the side of the car. As I watched him I thought, "I can do that, I can help mom with that." So a few days later while her car was parked in our driveway, I looked around and wouldn't you know... there was a hose! So I picked up the hose and I put it in the hole in the side of mom's car, just like the man at this other place had done. Well, it turns out that he was putting *gas* in her car, but I was putting in *water*. (Oops!) My heart was there and I really wanted to help mom, and so I filled her tank all the way up—with water.

Fortunately, I lived to tell about it, and the car was okay too. You know, that's just me, always trying to do a good job. I'm an over-achiever. What can I say?

I've gained some experience since that day and today I'm an ASE Master Technician. ASE stands for Automotive Service Excellence and is our industry's credentialing organization. You should make sure that anyone who works on your vehicle is ASE certified. It gives you confidence knowing that they've received the proper training to service your vehicle and have the education needed to work on today's vehicles.

I also have a degree in Automotive Service, which I earned from ASA, the Automotive Service Association, and their management institute.

My mom taught me to work hard and that learning and education never stops. And to stay on the cutting edge with the technology that runs today's vehicles, my staff and I are constantly going to classes and training events . We do this to keep ourselves sharp, and that allows us to service our customers with excellence and be their trusted source for information and expert repair service.

The Early Years

Leaning to treat customers right all started with my mom. I can remember the kind of worker that my mom was, and I think that's where it all began.

My mom was a single mom with three children. When I was about a fifth grader, I remember coming home from school at three o'clock and my mom arrived home shortly after five from her day job. We would have dinner together and then she would take a nap. She would wake up in time to tuck me in bed and then go to her night job at eleven o'clock and work until the morning.

The World's Best Waitress

My earliest memories of my mom are those of her being an extremely hard worker. I remember her working as a waitress at Denny's. She had a lot on her plate and learned that treating her customers well was very

Mike's mom is featured in the company brochure.

important. This is where my understanding of customer service began as well. So when I think about customer service, the thing that my mom taught me is not just hard work, but to really "own" the needs of the customer.

That means that you need to really have the word "empathy" in your vocabulary *and* in your actions. When we have empathy in our mind and in our actions, we can put ourselves in the customer's shoes, and ask, "What is their greatest need?" and then consider what resources we have to meet that need. We can then begin to pull out those resources to help meet that need.

Scan this to watch The Auto Guy's mom tell the rest of the story.

As we grow in our businesses, we need to continue to grow in our resources so that we can continue to meet needs. Our businesses need to meet the personal needs of every customer each time they come in. So what that means is that every time a customer comes in they're going to have different needs, their state of mind is going to be different, and what they've just gone through in the last week is going to be different. I need to make sure that I take the time to see where their needs are for that day, and look for ways to meet those needs, whether those needs relate directly to my business or not.

Let's say we received a call from a customer whose car is broken down on the side of the road. They really need two things: (1) they need their car taken care of – that's why they called in the first place, and (2) they also have other needs since they hadn't planned on this happening. There is probably someplace they were going besides the side of the road. The first thing we'll handle is getting the tow truck expedited. Next, and more importantly, we will help that customer get to where they were going. The best way to do that is to send someone after them and take them wherever they need to go (we have a FREE customer shuttle to do this very thing).

Another example of meeting the customer's needs is when a customer is out of town and they've left their car at our shop while they were gone. Since they are coming back into town over the weekend, wouldn't it be nice if, when they get home, their car were waiting for them in their driveway rather than at Parkway Automotive? They might need it Monday morning, so we would deliver their car back to their home so their car is where they're used to seeing it when they get home from their trip.

We work very diligently to know our customers and understand their needs so that we can provide them with amazing customer service. We've found that when we do this, our customers not only appreciate our efforts, their trust in us goes up significantly and they refer their friends to us. That's how our business has continued to grow for many years. And it all started with my mom.

More Than Repairing Cars

There's a word that many people don't like, but is a part of every business. That word is "sales." Sales are a part of every job of every business for anybody that does anything. I mean, I can't think of a single industry that everybody involved is not part of sales at some level. But when communicating with the customer one-on-one, be it eyeball to eyeball or on the phone, the job of the sales person is really **a transfer of beliefs** or ideas from one person to another. It's not trying to make the person buy something they don't want to buy or to "get sold"; it's **a transfer of beliefs.**

By having the technical background that I possess, I'm able to communicate to the customer, not just that they need a widget, but <u>why</u> they need a widget, and how it will benefit them to have the widget. For me, I must also believe in that widget, own that widget, use that widget for my own vehicles; not just have the knowledge to talk about it. For example, I would not want to talk with a consumer about having their transmission flushed every sixty thousand miles if I were not doing that on my own vehicle, my wife's vehicle and my children's vehicles. That's a belief system, because I know the transmission will last longer by having the fluid changed in it on a regular basis. That's the belief system that I have, so I'm able to communicate with my customer because I know why their transmission ought to be flushed.

It's really a matter of trust and integrity with me. I'm not going to recommend you do something that I'm not doing myself.

"Owning" the Call

If there's one thing that drives me crazy, or gives me great concern, is when I call a business and the person on the other end says, "Thank you for calling. To whom may I direct your call?"

This communicates to me that they can't, or don't want to, help me! It's as if somehow I'm supposed to know where it is I want them to transfer me and who it is at their company (whom I don't yet know) that is supposed to be able to answer my question or solve my problem. That's an all-too-often scenario that I encounter.

Another scenario is when I call and they answer the phone and I say the name of someone who works there. They reply, "Hold on just a minute please." I hear a "click" and they put me on hold. I may have been able to get the information I needed from the person answering the phone, but I thought I was talking to John when it was really Joe that picked up the phone. I say, "John?" and he says "No, click"—never asking if there is something he can answer for me or help me with.

So in both scenarios I just described, if we "own" the phone call, what we would say to the customer is:

> "Thank you for calling Parkway Automotive.
> This is Mike. How may I help you?"

And then there should be a pause to listen to understand what their needs are (back to meeting the needs of our customer). Many times you can assist that caller if you sincerely listen to them; and often you can do this without them having to be transferred to another person. Sometimes it can be as simple as taking a message. And when a message is taken from a customer on the phone, the message should be taken and then you should say to that customer,

> "My name is Mike. I will be sure that
> John gets this message."

THAT is what I call "owning" the call. And it adds great value to the person on the other end of the phone because you are treating them with respect and doing everything you can to meet their needs.

How many times do you call a business and you're not really confident that the person taking your information is <u>really</u> going to get your message to the person who needs it? So at Parkway what we want to do before we end any phone call is to be sure we tell the customer who we are and that we're going to make sure that the person they were calling for gets the message.

Now sometimes we do put the customer on hold. And when that needs to happen we should:

1. Ask for permission to put the caller on hold, and

2. Reassure them that if the person they're asking for isn't able to get to the phone in a reasonable amount of time, then we'll pick up the line again. We won't just leave the caller on the phone in an eternal hold mode.

Most phone systems have some type of an alarm to alert you when someone's been on hold for a long period of time. That is still <u>your</u> phone call until the other person picks it up – YOU "own" it. So you should do everything you can to meet the needs of that customer without transferring them to someone else. That is "owning" the phone call. It is your phone call until their need has been resolved or they've been connected to another person. It's your responsibility. So that's how we "own" the phone call.

At the end of the day, it *is* your customer because they are all customers of your business. And that's what I mean when I say that everybody is in sales. Without sales, there would be no business. <u>And a big part of sales is meeting the customer's needs and treating them with respect.</u>

The one thing every customer looks for in a business relationship is **trust**. And everything you can do to communicate trust will benefit your company. So when I can show the customer that I care about them by asking permission to put them on hold, coming back to the phone call after a reasonable amount of time, or assuring them I will deliver a message, I'm building trust. These seemingly little things, including what I mentioned earlier (taking the car back to their home when they're out of town or going to pick them up on the side of the road when their car is broken down), all work together to communicate "I care." And embedded in "I care" is the message, "You can trust me." And that's how we have tried to build our business at Parkway Automotive. In fact, every business owner in this book thinks just like I do.

Whether you are buying flowers, insurance, IT services, printing or you want to write your own book!

What I Like About Doing Business in Little Rock

I was born in Little Rock. I moved around a little bit, but I certainly call Arkansas my home and Little Rock my city. I attended McClellan High School here in Little Rock, and graduated from Van Buren High School. I think the thing that's really great about Little Rock is that the types of people you find in Little Rock are <u>friendly</u> people.

You can still find people in Little Rock who are willing to go a little bit deeper than "shallow" when it comes to conversation. They want you to talk with them about their dog or their children or their church or their kids' soccer team (or if you're talking with Roger Best—his car), things like that, not to mention the Razorback's—just mention them to Jason Everett and you'll have a friend for life. But that's what I'm talking about. It's very easy to get to know people here and that makes doing business in Little Rock a lot more fun.

The front porch of Parkway Automotive is a great place to sit and have some coffee.

Little Rock is also a city with technology. We have companies like Acxiom, Verizon, AT&T, Southwest Power Pool, Windstream, and Dillard's, along with Wal-Mart and Tyson in the state. We have large companies… and small companies. We are a town with technology, and we are also a community with people who don't mind sitting down and having a cup of tea with you, or coffee, or whatever you prefer. That's what I think makes

www.BigBusinessInLittleRock.com

Little Rock unique; it is the kind of people you'll find—both technologically advanced on one hand and old style "let's sit and talk on the front porch" on the other hand. Yes, people still do that and I think that's what I really enjoy about living and doing business in Little Rock.

Why Parkway Automotive?

With so many options available for vehicle repair, why should you choose Parkway Automotive?

Well, I want to start by saying that the one reason you would want to do business with Parkway Automotive is the people who work here. That's #1.

You're going to find people here you can trust. You're going to find people who know what it means to "own" the phone call and who will provide *Service That Will Amaze You*. My Team does this by really caring and having empathy for your situation and they are genuinely trying to help you solve whatever issue you may be having, whether it's general maintenance on your vehicle, or a major repair or electronic issue. You'll find people who have the knowledge, technology and empathy to get you answers on getting your car serviced.

After that, you'll discover that our philosophy on auto service is exactly like Roger Best with Biztek Connection. As we continue to monitor your vehicle's condition by having regular checkups by an ASE Certified technician, we are going to know *ahead of time* the things that need attention now and notify you of the things coming up to keep you and your family safe on the road. We provide this service through our **VIP Club** which entitles you to free oil changes, free tire rotations, and an inspection of your vehicle every 5,000 miles. It's fully transferrable from one car to the next without a transfer fee. You can find out more about our VIP Club at ParkwayAutomotive.net.

We also offer a **2-year, Unlimited mileage warranty** on the work that we do. We stand behind every repair for a full two years, no questions asked.

Finally, we have a **100% Risk Free Money Back Guarantee**, which means that after we've made three attempts to repair your vehicle, if we have not repaired it to your satisfaction, then we will give you one hundred percent of your money back. So there's <u>absolutely no risk</u> involved in having your car serviced at Parkway Automotive.

I assure you that when you bring your vehicle to Parkway Automotive, you'll experience the best of the best in Little Rock. In fact, we were voted "The Best of The Best in Little Rock" in 2012. We also received the "Ethics Award" from the Better Business Bureau, and in April 2012 I was featured on the cover of a national industry magazine—Ratchet & Wrench—and recognized for being in the Top 2% of independent repair shops in the nation. Being chosen to receive these types of awards is a real honor for my Team and me.

Currently, Parkway Automotive is the only repair shop in Little Rock, including all of the local dealerships, that's been approved by AAA Motor Club of North America. That says that we meet their standards. And those standards are re-inspected every 12 months both for our training and certification of all of our technicians, to our service advisors, to even the amount of insurance that we have. The lounge area must meet standards on how well it looks and how comfortable it is for our customers. All the services that a AAA member might expect, they're going to get when they come to Parkway Automotive.

Giving Back to the Community

I want to add another thought that I think is important for people to know. And that is about giving back. It's so important for businesses to give back, and what I'm really talking about is people giving back to people. Some of the ways that our company is involved, and our people are giving back, is through our support of the Arkansas Crisis Pregnancy Center. We support them by taking automobiles that someone doesn't want to repair, and we repair them, make them safe, and give them to the Crisis Pregnancy Center of Arkansas so that they can give them to one of their clients. This allows them to help moms who decided not to abort their child. These moms need help getting to the doctor, to work, and transporting their kids to school. We find this is a great way that we are able to contribute.

We also support a few elementary schools by giving back to the schools through the PTA Whenever a parent or grandparent has their vehicle service at Parkway Automotive, we give a portion of the labor sales back to their school's PTA. This assists the teachers with school supplies and other needs that benefit their students. Additionally, we recognize a "Teacher of the Month" at a local elementary school in conjunction with Ted Lewis at Floral Express Flower Market (a co-author of this book).

I also serve with Pulaski Technical College and on the Board of Directors for the Little Rock Better Business Bureau. I believe it's important to be involved in the community and make sure people are having their needs met. A great community is not just about good business; it's about strong education in our schools as well. That's why I enjoy being involved and giving back in so many ways. In fact, all of the businesses represented in this book give back to the community in some way. So when you decide to spend your money and time with us, it doesn't benefit some national headquarters. It benefits the community you love and live in.

How I Became "The Auto Guy" (the rest of the story)

In 1999 I started advertising on a local Christian radio station. One day, Jason Harper from a local television station, KATV Channel 7, heard one of my ads. He contacted me about doing a segment for Channel 7 on winterizing a car. I completed that segment and the producers liked what they saw, so they invited me back a couple of times. Soon after, they asked me to be on every week, and that was the birth of "The Auto Guy".

I was on Channel 7 for over 10 years. Viewers would call in and ask questions about their car and I would answer them live on-air. It was a fun time for me and really kept me on my toes. I had to use everything I had learned up to that point to ensure I was giving these people the right information that they could trust.

This was such a great experience for me that I may do again sometime. I think people liked the idea of having someone they could ask questions of and build a relationship with—even if it was through a TV show. People like to do business with people they know, like and trust. Becoming "The Auto Guy" helped me to build those types of relationships with many in our community. Go to YouTube and search "The Auto Guy Parkway Automotive" (or scan this QR code with your smart phone) and you will see my smiling face.

Summing It All Up

I've always called Little Rock my home. My roots are here and they are very deeply entrenched in this Southern soil. Like a mature oak tree, I've been able to endure a number of storms through the years. My success comes not from my own effort alone, but is built on the foundational teaching I received from my mom, the opportunities afforded me by others, and the loyalty and trust given to me by the people of this great city.

I can think of no other place that I'd rather live and do business. I have visited a number of cities in my time and I'm here to tell you that Little Rock is one of the finest BIG "little" cities in America. I'm proud to call it my home.

A Special Offer

As a Big Business in Little Rock reader, I'd like to extend an opportunity for you to experience for yourself what doing business with Parkway Automotive is like. Just for you, I'd like to offer you an experience—not just some oil change.

Simply copy this coupon and bring it with you (or bring in this book and I'll sign it for you).

Little Rock is my home and 100% of your money stays in this "Little" city.

$25.00 Any Service

Parkway Automotive
708 Kirk Road
Little Rock, AR | 501-821-6111
www.ParkwayAutomotive.net

Cannot be combined with other offers.
One Coupon per Customer   Code: BBinLR

About Mike "The Auto Guy"

Mike Davidson opened Parkway Automotive in January 1997. He's an ASE Master Certified Technician and was the Napa ASE Technician of the Year in Arkansas 6 years in a row. He serves on the board of directors for the Arkansas Better Business Bureau was recently featured on the cover of Ratchet and Wrench Magazine. Mike and Nancy, his wife of 23 years, have four children. They attend The Bible Church of Little Rock and are passionate followers of Jesus Christ.

J. Ted Lewis

FLORAL EXPRESS
Flower Market Since 1989

www.BigBusinessInLittleRock.com

The Key to Success

As an elderly lady drove up to one of the two service windows I noticed an overnight bag in her back seat but gave it no thought until she handed me a key.... "Young man, I am on my way to the hospital for a short stay later today, please duplicate this key for me. It will be for my neighbor to have access to my house while I am in the hospital." Without hesitation, I asked if she wanted to wait or drive back thru in a few minutes. She stated she needed to run another errand and would return.

Floral Express Premiere Drive-thru was in the parking lot of a local hardware store (our first drive-thru location had been a previous Kodak Film Developing Kiosk, then a Key Duplication Kiosk). I simply walked in the hardware store, had the key duplicated and $2.35 later, I returned to the kiosk awaiting the return of my newest customer.

As she drove up to the window I greeted her with a smile and said,

"I have your key ready. We normally do not duplicate keys; we're a florist, but I saw your need and wanted to help you, so I just had your key duplicated at the hardware store behind you."

Though our store was quite eye catching with the bright color flowers, plants and balloons that I had outside that day she exclaimed, "I had no idea! Thank you so much!" as I handed her keys through the window.

"Well, I might as well purchase a basket of pretty flowers for my hospital stay," she stated as she was looking for her wallet.

Now it was my turn to provide what Floral Express does best. Beautiful flowers with over the top customer service!

I don't know the outcome of her hospital stay...but I learned early on that providing service—not just any service—but OUTRAGEOUS service was going to be the strong suit in building my new endeavor.

The Road to Little Rock

My life had been going through a lot of turmoil while I was living in Atlanta, Georgia. I decided it was time for a change. As I have matured, I've realized that home *really is* where your heart is.

My parents had left Arkansas and moved to Tennessee for a few years. When they decided to return to Arkansas they chose to settle in Little Rock, the state capitol.

I had never lived in Little Rock or knew much about it other than it being the financial hub of Arkansas. I thought, "It's the largest city in Arkansas, so maybe I won't lose the big city feel that I had grown accustomed to in Atlanta." I was in for a pleasant surprise.

Holiday Inn Corporate had been good to me. I had been their Human Resources Director for the Crowne Plaza in Atlanta. When I decided to relocate, I started applying for positions at local hotels in Little Rock and quickly found that I was over qualified. Little Rock was a much smaller market than I had realized for professionals with my qualifications.

My first clue was when, just 2 weeks earlier, as I drove into Little Rock on I-40 from Memphis, I quickly approached North Little Rock, with interstate lanes approaching from several different directions. Thoughts of how large this city was quickly disappeared as I approached the ramp for my exit onto I-630.

Six lanes are merging in one direction..."pretty good sized financial district," I thought, but those lanes quickly shrank to three lanes. I remembered my parents telling me that I would drive through downtown and a few short miles later I would exit University Avenue. As I blindly drove past the University exit (I was still looking for downtown!!) I reached the end of I-630. "An interstate that comes to an end???" It was *then* that I realized that the 2 or 3 tall buildings I had seen a few minutes earlier *was* downtown!

Who would have thought *that* would have been the beginning of a lifetime of memories in one of the finest cities I have ever known?!?!

Everything but the Groom

As my relentless hunt for employment continued, I re-worked my resume with a simpler overview. Hopeful that employment would be right around the corner, I learned that my mom had started a business as a full-service wedding consultant; she called it Precious Memories. Her energy and enthusiasm about this new threshold in her life was very contagious. She was booking wedding events daily. I'll never forget her slogan:

"We provide everything but the groom."

Wedding gowns, catering, cakes, venues, honeymoon destinations, limos and flowers. I was proud of her and was glad to see her "little" part-time business doing so well. I wanted to share her excitement yet knew I needed to find employment of my own.

I finally got a call from a local hotel, The Camelot, and became their human resources director. It was a short venture with this property. Three months later I learned that Marriott Corporation was coming to Little Rock with their first property—The Courtyard. As I was standing in the lobby of The Camelot, two gentlemen approached me and asked if they could speak to the HR Director. After introductions and pleasantries I told them they were. We had dinner that evening and in two short weeks I began my career with Marriott Hotels.

Mom's wedding consultation business had a continual difficulty soliciting retail flower shops to help her with her wedding floral work. They felt she was taking business away from them when, in fact, she was trying to give them business.

All she was wanting was a 10, 12, or 15% "finder's fee" for bringing them the business. Through her frustration one evening, when she had eight or nine weddings booked with no florist, I made a statement that would change the course of my life,

"It can't be that hard."

Twenty-five years later, I'm living that statement.

Mom had a friend who worked as a part-time florist who said to me, "You want to give it a whirl?" And I said, "Sure!" I still had about 3 months left on my tenure at Marriott and I'd told them that I was branching out into this floral part of my life. After working with my mom's friend for about two weeks, she told Mom, "Ted's not going to have any problem; he has a natural God given talent." All I needed to learn was a few tricks of the trade and I was well on my way.

Well, I was able to knock out the next eight or nine weddings for Mom fairly easily. I was able to provide everything from Bridal bouquets, boutonnieres, and altar arrangements to throwaway bouquets, reception arrangements, and the whole nine yards. During this time I had a thought, "Well, I need a space," because I wanted to do something a bit different.

A Kodak® Moment

In the span of about 6 or 7 months (I'd already turned in my notice at Marriott and turned down the opportunity of going to Dallas to work for them) I knew this flower gig was going to end up being something that I wanted to do, probably just temporarily, but one never knows.

I never dreamed that I was going to let this be my career because this wasn't what I went to college for… but, I read every book, every design manual and started considering enrolling in the floral design classes offered across the country. Still, I wanted to do something a little bit different than any other flower shop.

One day I noticed that there was a kiosk available on the corner of Markham and Rodney Parham that had been sitting vacant for a few months. It was originally a photo film booth and then a key shop, and then just sat empty. So I thought, "Why not create a drive-through florist? Why hasn't anybody thought about that? Why can't you just order flowers out of your car like you would order lunch from a drive thru?" After giving it a little bit of thought (not much mind you) I laid down $300 to rent this kiosk.

That night at dinner I told Mom and Dad and my brother,

> "Well, I have a retail space now
> and I want to open a florist shop."

I think everyone in the family thought I'd lost my mind.

We were a little building for 2 ½ years with 2 drive-thru windows. We were featured in several floral publications, and all of a sudden I was a hit being the drive-thru florist.

And so I became a speaker on a speaking circuit on how to market your business. I was teaching other floral shops novel and different ways to market their business and the drive-thru was a success! We became Arkansas' premier drive-thru florist, Floral *Express*—that's how we got our name. You couldn't come in; you had to drive-thru.

A New Beginning

Mom kept her wedding consultation business for about 2 more years and she married another 30 to 40 brides in that span of time. She was the only wedding consultant in the yellow pages back then. If you look at the yellow pages now, it has 4 or 5 pages full of consultants, so she was sort of breaking the barrier on that industry. So Floral *Express* became a type of wedding and event planning center. Even though our size was very small, we were still able to pull things off because we did all the floral work at the event sites or the venues.

Two years later we opened a retail store on Cantrell. This was a much larger location of about 1,800 square feet – it was so large compared to the kiosk that I felt like I'd died and gone to Heaven! We went from 150 square feet to 1,800 square feet and we still kept our drive-thru. From there I could see that the Hotel industry and human resources career was in my rear view mirror. I probably wouldn't be going back to that, but those skills helped me hire staff of up to 42 employees, and we grew to 5 stores in a matter of about 15 years.

I had a family member in every store, and then Mom and Dad decided they were ready to retire. My sister-in-law was finishing nursing school and was ready to get out of the "family business" as well, so we began selling and closing stores as leases came up. Fortunately, this all happened before the economy went "south," which I think was really an answer to prayer. I think God knew what he was putting me through and knew that I didn't need to be faced with the burden of multiple stores and staff when the economy tanked.

The World Within Reach

So now I'm down to one location, which is in downtown Little Rock (the same downtown that I had missed a few years earlier) in a 40-story office building that houses anywhere from 3,000 to 3,500 people who are employed in a variety of businesses. It's like we're in our own little city with our own captive audience.

After we closed the multiple locations, I retained the name 'Floral *Express*' but we've added 'Flower Market' to it.

We're part of a worldwide network of about 30,000 florists. And because of these relationships, you're able to call me as late as one or 2 o'clock in the afternoon (depends on what the time zone is and where the flowers are going) but we can simply hit a few buttons on a computer and your order is gone. A flower shop in our network receives your order and they design and duplicate it as close as they can with the flowers that are available in that particular region of the world. In a matter of hours your flowers are delivered. **Boom! Flowers delivered the same day almost anywhere in the USA. International deliveries may take up to 48 hour delivery depending upon the time zone.** (We're probably faster at delivering flowers than Sir Speedy is in printing your business cards, but don't tell Mike Bennett that!)

The Creative Genius Behind Floral Express

Every flower shop has their own creativity and their own "brand" that they are promoting. At Floral *Express*, we pride ourselves in having the freshest flowers possible. We use a local vendor in order to help support the local economy, yet we also understand that even our local vendors can't get some of the flowers that our customer desires.

To serve our customers and give them the finest variety, we can order flowers from flower farms in South America, Holland, Hawaii, California, Canada and a variety of exotic locations around the world, and still have your flowers delivered the next day.

So, we pride ourselves on some of the freshest flowers, and we get shipments of fresh flowers 3 times a week. That's pretty fresh, which means that when you order flowers from Floral *Express* Flower Market, you're **guaranteed** an easy 7 to 14 days of beauty and freshness, depending on the variety of flowers.

The common misperception that "flowers don't last very long" is really a misunderstanding. When you consider the impact flowers can make on someone's day, the memory they will have and the beauty they bring, you begin to understand that flowers last a lot longer than giving someone a steak dinner or bottle of wine.

And it's the emotional value and the impact that flowers have. I'm a firm believer that if more men sent flowers, there would be fewer problems in marriages and less divorce in our world. If a woman says "Oh, that's just a waste of money," all she's telling you is 'sending me flowers is going to take our relationship to the next level.' It's a type of "code" that they use to see how perceptive we are (I've learned that being in the floral industry this long!)

> Next year, instead of flowers, try sending her a toaster or a vacuum cleaner on her birthday or Valentine's Day—that won't work!

But a bouquet of flowers and a box of chocolates communicate to her that you really are thinking about her and you care. Many men believe that flowers are a "feminine thing," but what you're saying is that you are thinking about her; you're thinking about her emotions and her feelings and so when you step into a flower shop or even take a moment to call a flower shop, that's letting her know that you really are thinking about her.

Each time I call Ted at Floral Express Flower Market for flowers, I can be assured of the freshest and prettiest designs for my home and guests.

- Gail Arnold

And who doesn't love chocolate?!? We specialize in a lot of chocolates; Godiva is one of our finest, along with those from the 'Sweet Shop.' 'Sweet Shop' does some of the best handmade truffles you can enjoy; they're absolutely excellent and come in several different flavors. A lot of flower shops don't have the extensive gourmet line that we do in chocolates and truffles and pretzels and the pralines and the turtles and the brags and all those wonderful things that people like to enjoy (is your mouth watering yet???).

Beauty by Design

All our designers are certified. They've attended the Arkansas Master Florist School, which means they're graduates of an extensive learning program. This is why Floral *Express* Flower Market has the most trendy, up-to-date design styles in Little Rock.

When you order flowers for a bouquet, a birth, wedding, funeral or any special occasion, you want it to be fresh and beautiful. That's why we are constantly staying up on the latest fashions and trends. Giving flowers is an extension of you. You can trust us to make you look good.

Here Comes The Bride

Ever since my mom started her wedding consulting business, I've come to believe that the florist ought to be one of the first contacts that a bride-to-be makes when beginning to plan her wedding. Why? Because the florist has all the contacts the bride will need to make her day as perfect as can be. I mean, even to the point that we can refer you to recommended bridal shops that sell wedding gowns. We have a veritable Rolodex® simply because we do so many weddings. We also know which are reputable and the ones you'd rather avoid. We can also direct you to a jewelry store, a bakery, and can give you the folks who have received the highest honors, who are the reader's choice awards, who really pull through and care about the wedding. And planning a wedding a year out is not too soon to get started. A year goes pretty fast. Now, I wouldn't get started any sooner than that, besides perhaps reserving your venue (and we can even help you with that). You may not want to have your wedding in a church. You may want to have it outdoors. You may want to have it in a hall somewhere or country club. But a year out is OK to get started on that. On the other hand, we have even pulled weddings off within a week. I don't recommend that, but it can be done when needed. We are Floral *Express*, you know.

====================================
Begin your wedding planning online
at the website we created just for brides:
www.YourLuxuryEvent.com.
====================================

I recall a story from the drive-thru. We were just getting started with our Kiosk when a Cadillac Sedan convertible pulled up with two couples in the car and they wanted a bridal bouquet. I thought they were ordering one for the future, but no… they were heading off to the Justice of the Peace right then. So I quickly put a bridal bouquet together and a boutonniere and they were gone. That's *Express* service.

Fifteen years later, this young lady and 2 toddlers came into our store on Cantrell. I was standing at the front counter and she said, "Ted?" and I said, "Yes." "Do you remember me?" I looked at her and I said, "No, I'm sorry. I don't." She said, "Do you remember a Cadillac Sedan convertible pulling up to your drive thru on Rodney Parham and Markham about 15 years ago?" And I answered, "Oh yeah, yeah, they were going to get married at the Justice of the Peace." She said, 'I'm that bride!"

"Oh my goodness, that's awesome!" I replied. So we visited for a few minutes, then I realized the relationships that you can build in this business because of the impact that you have on their lives. It's that whole impact of flowers that really make memories for folks and for someone to hunt me down after 15 years to say "Thank you!"... Now *that's* customer service and that's building relationships with your customer.

That's really what Floral *Express* is about—helping you build relationships and making it easy for you to buy flowers for your loved ones. We make you look good by making the process of ordering flowers simple... as simple as a phone call or simply logging on to our website (www.floralx.com). In a couple of minutes you're order is complete and your flowers are on their way.

Of course, if you are already a customer of ours, then all your information is on file, so it's even faster. We keep everything private and secure. We don't share our database with anyone and we can keep your credit card information in a secure file to make it even easier for you to order. You can be anywhere in the world and give us a call or click on our website and BOOM! it's done—your flowers are on their way. I've had a customer just holler at me while I'm out and about, "Hey Ted, would you please send my wife flowers tomorrow?" That's all I need to serve one of our loyal customers.

The Royal Treatment

Another way we serve our customers is through our free Royalty Rewards program. Every time you make a purchase, you earn points. Those points can then be redeemed as cash for a future purchase. It's a great way for you to save money when sending flowers and making someone else feel special. There's no cost – ever – to participate, and <u>every purchase earns you more money</u>. I think we're the only floral shop in Arkansas providing this type of benefit to our customers. Just another way that Floral *Express* is staying on the leading edge and adding value to our loyal customers.

All in a Days Work

Recently one of our loyal customers—a law firm—sent their event coordinator in (we'll call her Amy). She needed help with a corporate event. They wanted to promote their evening at The Arkansas Repertory Theatre here in Little Rock. Since they sponsor this each year, we're familiar with what they like to do and always come up with creative ideas for them. Amy came in and simply said,

> "Ted, here's the invitation. The show is Treasure Island, what can you all do for us?"

In a matter of 20 minutes, my staff and I came up with this great idea of using pirates, treasure chests, and flowers on the buffets. Amy was thrilled with our idea, told us to "handle it" and turned and walked out. BOOM! As fast as she had entered, she was out of there. That's the type of customer experience you can expect from our staff.

I've found over the years that a lot of people over complicate events. Amy's vision of Treasure Island was exactly what we had envisioned and we got it all done in about 20 to 30 minutes. I'm not saying every event can be done that quickly, but we had worked with her for the last 10 years so we sort of knew what she would like.

The most common mistake I find in planning a corporate event is *over* planning. Amy's event for Treasure Island was happening in just 2 weeks—BOOM! It's done!! Someone can come to us a year out for an event (like a wedding) and all we need to know is the table count and your theme and BOOM! It's done. We'll handle everything else.

You don't have to worry yourself with all of the little details, just give us what you want, give us your colors and your theme and we'll handle the rest of it. We're professionals and that's what we do for a living.

But I understand... I mean, how many times do you get married in life? Hopefully just once. And since you have never done this before, I can understand being anxious and wanting to make sure that everything is right. That's why we strive so hard to build trust with our customers. We've found that building that loyalty and trust with a customer makes planning any event a lot easier, whether it's for a wedding, a birth or even a funeral.

Regardless of the event, Floral *Express* Flower Market is here to deliver the freshest, most beautiful arrangement of flowers you can imagine. From a simple corsage, to a funeral arrangement, to a full-blown wedding, we are here to make your life easier. Just call us (501-666-3196) or order from our website (www.floralx.com).

Loving this "Little" City

I'm thankful that I didn't keep driving those many years ago. Although our downtown may not be the largest in the States, it's most definitely a vibrant city that offers abundant opportunities for small business to thrive. The River Market is a fabulous area full of restaurants, museums and unique stores—there's really nothing else quite like it (you can ask Roger Best about that). And watching the Travelers at Dickey-Stephens Field is a terrific way to enjoy an evening with friends and family.

Little Rock offers abundant opportunities for those with ambition and an open mind. The people are friendly, the cultural activities plentiful, and the business climate is positive and inviting.

I never thought I'd be running a premier floral shop in one of the best cities in America. But one never can tell where the road is going to take you. Let me encourage you to take a chance (as I did renting the Kiosk) and live your dream. You may struggle a bit at first, but as you persevere you'll find that living and working here comes with a number of hidden benefits and blessings. Though I started small, I believe Floral *Express* Flower Market truly has become a BIG Business in Little Rock.

A Special Offer:

Order your flowers for your next fundraising event from Floral *Express* Flower Market and we will add 10% to the cause.

You can choose to either add flowers equal to 10% of the total order, take 10% off of your event order, or you can pay for your order in full and we'll write you a check for 10% of the total amount.

We love doing business in Little Rock and this is just one way we can give back to this great "little" city.

Mike Bennett

Sir Speedy®
Printing and Marketing Services

A Wise Use of Talents

I grew up in Wichita, Kansas, and had a wonderful childhood. My brother, sister and I were blessed with a mother and father that worked hard, disciplined us consistently, taught us about life in the here and now and what lies waiting in eternity, and loved us unconditionally. As an added advantage my father was a creative man and very entrepreneurial.

Early in life I had the opportunity to see a great example of a man who was always aspiring to do more. He was a man who was eager to use his talents wisely and he didn't want to waste them. As a result, I had a multitude of opportunities to learn about business and even had the opportunity to work with him in several small businesses. Some failed, some succeeded, and although I witnessed the many joys and disappointments, all of it was used to teach me and mold me into the man I am today.

Little Rock, Arkansas, came into my life in 1984. My father took a position with the University of Arkansas for Medical Sciences and the entire family made a very big move. I had completed two years of my college education at Wichita State University but moved with the family and transferred to the University of Arkansas at Little Rock. After one semester, I moved back to Wichita to complete my education and graduated from WSU in 1987.

Returning to Little Rock for visits while in college, I became very familiar with Little Rock and developed a love for the city and the people here who had become my friends. And, since Little Rock is where my family had grown roots, it was an easy decision to move here upon graduation. As an added incentive my father and I had developed a business idea while I was in school that we wanted to further develop. My move here was most definitely a good decision and I have no regrets!

A Little Business That Grew

Anxious to spread my wings and make some money, I started a small design business shortly after I moved to Little Rock in 1987. As one would expect, it was a small start designing a few logos, newspaper and magazine advertisements, brochures and the like for a small group of clients that I was introduced to through some very helpful and loving friends. Some of those clients I began working with in 1987 are still clients to this day!

However, at that point in time, and as my circle of contacts grew, I was given the opportunity to work for one of the more creative advertising agencies in the city as a production artist. Although I loved the idea of being in business for myself, the allure of "secure" income and a consistent paycheck drew me towards full-time employment. With the experience gained through that job, I was able to join another agency as a designer. I enjoyed working with the staff at both agencies but deep inside, I still had the desire to be in business for myself. The opportunity to join forces with another gentleman I had met through my freelancing days allowed me to take a step back towards being the entrepreneur I feel I was meant to be. And that is where I find myself 25 years later—operating two companies in the same field that complement each other very nicely—Bennett Design Group and Sir Speedy Printing and Marketing Services.

The differences between Bennett Design Group and Sir Speedy Printing and Marketing Services might seem obvious, but I view each as key pieces of the same puzzle. Bennett Design Group is responsible for coming up with the creative concepts and the crafting of design and artwork. It is where ideas are generated and developed and ultimately designed in a manner that works.

Then Sir Speedy Printing takes over with the execution and fulfillment of the creative process. Both are integral to successful marketing, and both, if skillfully executed, complement each other.

Innate Design

Most printing facilities claim to have a design department and a designer on staff. And, true to their word, most printing companies have someone on the payroll that they call their designer. I've found that more likely than not, the designer on staff has simply worked themselves up from the guy who started at sixteen or seventeen sweeping the floors, running errands, a little bit of this or that, but had a knack for Photoshop or the latest graphics software. Many times, as a result of longevity, tenure, or convenience, people with little or no design skills are then entrusted with the position of designer.

This may cause friction with some, and it may sound mean-spirited, however, I am simply making the point that titles really mean very little—especially when talking about graphic design and the creative process.

The difference is in the talents that various designers possess and the measurable qualifications of the individuals that actually do the work. Quality of craftsmanship, ideas, and thought process are all vital components that can create a solid foundation for any product or service you choose to market or sell. A business owner must understand the differences and choose wisely who will represent their company in the marketplace—regardless of the size of their marketing budget!

Formal training has a tremendous amount to do with the final design of a piece. But, having been in this industry for over 25 years, I've found that very few people seeking a designer position, even with a college degree, would be hired by my company. I routinely pass by many applicants with a degree from some very reputable schools. We've hired a few, but what I've learned over the last 25+ years is:

the degree is great *if*
there was a solid foundation
to build upon from the beginning.

There's something intangible that I'm finding with talented designers. You can train to a certain level; you can teach, you can show, you can help, but unless there is that "something" there, you do reach the ceiling fairly quickly. I firmly believe that "something" is a God-given talent. It's a tough road if the raw talent is not there. That's one reason I appreciate Ted Lewis' team at Floral Express Flower Market (Ted is a co-author of this book). They are expert designers with a solid foundation. They have that "something" that is difficult to describe, but you know it when you see it.

I am very diligent at this point in my career to locate those individuals whom I believe not only have what it takes on paper, but have it mentally. They have the skill set, the desire, and have the work ethic to actually accomplish what our clients need. It is not a formula; it is something you are born with, that you develop over time. I'm very selective.

Good vs. Great

One of our goals and passions is to assist business owners to recognize the difference between good or mediocre design and great design. The advantages of great design in marketing can make a tremendous difference in the ultimate success of those efforts. It's really more important than many business owners may think.

For example, great design oftentimes has little to do with personal taste. I believe that there is order to the world in which we live. Obviously, you will also find chaos and disorder. And there are many things that are absolute—rock solid. Things we simply count on every day and often take for granted such as gravity, air, the sun rising and setting, etc. There are also intangible absolutes that I believe we know as a human being—things we innately discern as right or wrong, good or bad, pleasing or unpleasing. I try to bring that sense of order into design.

There are design styles that are chaotic, disorganized, and radically unstructured and they have their place in communication if used properly. But the vast majority of the time, we are looking for structure and stability. <u>As a designer I am always looking for visual and conceptual relationships that bring that sense of stability into the messages our clients want to present</u>.

Ironically most of the time the stability that we are looking for comes down to the small details—visually and conceptually. What I've learned and what I've been able to teach our designers is that great design can be distilled down to the simple and proper ordering of design elements.

When proper attention is given to the creative process, great design follows, and that is what we seek to provide our clients. If done well, our clients can very quickly understand the point of the copy, the graphics, and the information we want them to see. Their intended message quickly comes to the forefront because there's order to the underlying foundation.

Our designers understand that the subtle things in design make the difference between well-crafted and sloppy design. A lot of the design in our society comes close to being good, but close isn't the same as great. We have a young man on our staff that I am currently instructing in our design methods. He is a very talented designer, but still very young in understanding and experience. It has been exciting for me to see him "get it" as he presents his work to me, and together we tweak just a few things that would seem very insignificant on the surface. Sometimes it's just one or two elements in the design, but other times it's a whole page of items that are moved a fraction of an inch or even fractions of a point in many cases, and in doing so the page gains a stronger sense of order and stability. I am fully convinced that when that design is viewed by its intended audience, they will react in a much more positive manner than if we had just settled for mediocrity.

Obviously, we still place a very high value on our client's ideas and preferences. We desire to use their ideas, color schemes, logos, graphic images, etc. with great design as our goal. The things I have written so far are very concrete in my mind. That being said, there is still a tremendous amount of "gray area" that gives us the freedom and flexibility to be creative and to give individual style and individual flare based on the likes or dislikes of our client. As solid as a design may be, if our client does not like it, we have not done our job!

Start Here

Over the years we have set ourselves up to be the one source for anything to do with marketing a business. It didn't used to be that way. I learned the design and marketing business at a time when an illustrator was engaged for one aspect of a project, a typographer would be sourced to set type, and if you needed a photograph, you would hire a photographer to shoot a specific photo to exactly fit your needs. There could be as many as six to eight people involved with their own individual specialties that would come together to put a project together.

With advances in technology, computers, and software, the design process has changed tremendously. Most printers have set themselves up, or at least tried to set themselves up, to be a one-stop shop that can handle everything. I would say most of them would come close until you consider what we've just been discussing—the design side of the business. At that point, most of them fall desperately short.

Bamboo Fly Rods to Billion Dollar Businesses

Martin/Darrell

We love working with businesses of all sizes. In fact, one fun project from the past involved a small start-up business with a gentleman who was selling bamboo fly rods out of his garage. He was a true craftsman and his finished products were absolutely beautiful! Although the odds were that he was never going to be the next Bass Pro Shops®, it was a blast coming up with a logo and business cards that he could distribute at the various trade shows and events around the country that he frequented selling hand crafted bamboo fly rods.

Just as he did, I would encourage any business owner to visit with us in the early stages of their marketing development. Getting us involved from the beginning provides the best opportunity for us to offer the most assistance. And we strongly stress that the size of the budget does not necessarily determine whether or not we can assist a potential client. We've assisted many clients with smaller budgets that simply wanted to establish a word mark that really wouldn't even be classified as a logo—just simple typography treatments to get their business rolling. On the other hand, our largest client is a multi-billion dollar corporation based in Virginia. They have multiple operating companies around the country and we've had the pleasure of working with many of those as well providing everything from heavy print design and large format printing, vehicle wraps, to creative concepts and campaigns. We also assisted the Little Rock location with a trade show for several hundred restaurateurs held in Hot Springs, Arkansas. To us, it matters not how large or small the client is – we just want to be involved in assisting with great design!

Honestly, we feel like we've been gifted in the area of helping people hone and grow their ideas and dreams through design. Once that hard work is done, it's relatively easy to print it, and we even do that for our clients as well! If our client would like to have the logo placed on a nice polo or button-up shirt, we can facilitate that. If they need a website (which all businesses do) we do that as well! The design and ideas make the difference—from there we can handle the rest as well.

A Complete Library at Our Fingertips

One of the advantages of being in the creative business for as long as we have is our accumulation of knowledge and ideas. We have worked with so many clients from a vast array of industries that we possess a breadth of knowledge and experience very few companies have. It's as if we are able to go into a library of archives when searching for a concept or solution for a design project. There are so many resources available that we're sure to come out with something that we can work with. That is huge for the typical business owner needing creative assistance. Since they are focused on running a business and accomplishing their goals, the last thing they have time for is how to effectively market their venture.

We can readily assist based on decades of experience and ideas that we have at our fingertips. Even if all they can bring us is an initial idea, we can bring ideas to the table which enable us to help direct our client to a successful outcome. It's what we do every day and that's why we're a great place to start. It's all about communicating your message through great design.

22 Years in the Making

I had the privilege of working with a client on a new logo a few years ago. They were very pleased with the final logo and asked, "Just how long did it take you to do this logo for us?" I answered, "About twenty-two years." He chuckled and nodded and I knew he understood my point that his logo came about partially as a result of the years of experience I had gained up to that point. With a few more years added since then, it's almost second nature to me now. Don't get me wrong, every logo and design project brings its own unique challenges – and some are still very difficult. But just knowing where the best place to jump off and get going is something that can really only be gained through experience.

The exciting part of our business is that every client brings their own unique qualities to the table. Our experience allows us to peruse a vast library and start picking and pulling, choosing and constructing what it is that our new project needs. That translates into a tremendous advantage for our clients.

The Benefits of Little Rock

Little Rock is a great place to live, raise a family and conduct business. I love the size of Little Rock because it's not so large that I feel lost, but it's not so small that I know everybody. It's not uncommon to be in the grocery store and see a friend you haven't seen in a few years or even your next-door neighbor in the next aisle. Or if you're ever eating at one of the many restaurants in the River Market, you may run into Roger Best and his wife. I just love that about Little Rock.

I also like Little Rock because it's the capital city. There are a lot of wonderful things that happen here politically as a result of the various state associations that choose Little Rock as their business home.

I'm a firm believer in the "grow where you are planted" philosophy. As I decided to "plant" my family in Little Rock many years ago, I put down my roots and have entrenched my business and myself in this community. We support many local charities and non-profits each year and, hopefully, are making a big difference in the lives of our clients and those whom they serve.

The growth we've seen as a company has come from the growing roots in the fertile business soil in Little Rock. I'm sure I could have grown a business most anywhere, but I'm certainly thankful that I began my small business here and have watched it grow into a Big Business in Little Rock.

A Special Offer – Free Design and Printing Review

As a no-risk opportunity for anyone interested, we are offering a Free Design and Printing Review. The offer would include about an hour of consulting time to review the various printed materials used by a company and discuss any new ideas a business owner may have. We'll ask some questions, give some thoughts, get some ideas from you and you'll have no obligation to do business with us whatsoever.

Another Special Offer – 250 FREE Business Cards

Bring in your copy of *Big Business in Little Rock* and we'll design and print 250 business cards for you at no cost. Just ask for Mike!

Michael DeLon

90Day Author
Publish Your Book in 90 Days Without Writing a Sentence

A New Chapter

I was at a point in my career when I knew it was about time for a change. I walked to the library in my home and I pulled out one of my favorite marketing books. As I turned the pages I knew that this was my future. I was finally going to live my dream.

I love the world of marketing and advertising. It's a fascinating world that allows you to really apply your creative juices, to stand apart from your competition, and to learn how to communicate your message clearly and compellingly to a prospect so they will start doing business with you. I've read a lot of definitions for marketing and most of them are more confusing than clarifying. So, in order to provide some clarity for my clients, I came up with my own definition:

>Marketing is Everything You Do
>to GAIN and RETAIN a Customer.

When I walked into my library that day, I didn't pick up just any book. I looked for a book from one of my favorite marketing experts, Jay Abraham. He has been helping small business owners with their marketing and advertising for many, many years and has a great track record. But I would not know all of that, or who Jay was at all, unless he had published his book. And it's *because* he published a book that many now consider him an expert, including me.

So to whom do you turn for "expert advice?" When you have a question or a problem that you need to solve, or perhaps are facing a quandary for which you need some direction, where do you go? To whom do you turn? Who might you find on your library shelves that you consider an "expert" in your life?

We all have experts we turn to from time to time. They may be in your personal life concerning finances, insurance, and legal advice; or they may be in your professional life concerning process, time management, and sales. There's an expert in most every field, people like Bob Vila in home repair, or Jerry Baker with gardening, or Dave Ramsey for debt-free living, or the late Zig Ziglar for sales. They are all perceived as experts because they published a book—and now you can too.

90Day Author allows you to "Publish Your Book in 90 Days Without Writing a Sentence." We have developed a process whereby any business owner (who is really an expert at what s/he does anyway) can publish a physical book in 90 days without the hassle of laboring in front of a computer screen typing and editing. We've perfected a method that removes every barrier to publishing your book and allows you to retain all of the control, intellectual property rights, and profits. We are a "royalty-free" publisher focused on helping you grow your business.

We help you take your ideas and turn them into a book without you doing the writing. Our proprietary *Speak to Write* system is simple, easy and fast. You'll be amazed at how quickly you can get your ideas out of your head and onto the written page.

But writing a book is about a whole lot more than just having a book. So, at 90Day Author, we also provide you with marketing strategies to promote your book (and yourself) as an expert. This positions you uniquely in the market and will help you to **attract** new customers, **engage** more profitably with your current customers, **retain** existing customers, and **stimulate** referrals automatically.

<u>Having your own book is a marketing strategy that will separate you from your competition faster than any other medium.</u>
www.BigBusinessInLittleRock.com

Being Perceived as "The Expert"

When you hand a copy of your book to a prospect, you'll be able to have a one-on-one conversation with them *without* being present. Then, when you *do* have your first meeting, they will be pre-disposed to do business with you because they've been able to bond with you through the pages of your book. You'll have already "set the stage" and will have defined the "rules of engagement" so that they begin to "speak your vocabulary" (which we also help you create).

Plus, you'll have already answered many of their questions and overcome their purchasing resistance. Instead of being what Dan Kennedy calls "an unwelcome pest," you'll be positioned as a "welcome guest."

They will perceive you as the expert (because you wrote the book) and they'll desire to do business with *you* versus your competitors who only gave them a brochure. You'll very quickly gain market share and greater credibility. This all happens when you become an author and publish your book.

As a marketing strategist, my clients look to me to help position them in a "category of one" so they will be perceived differently from everyone else. Now, there are a variety of ways to do this, but the way I like best is to position my client as an expert in their field. This is because experts have more authority (what they say holds weight), they are more credible (the media loves to interview and get sound bites from experts who are credible sources), and they are called upon for their expertise in their chosen field. Without question, the fastest, easiest, and most profitable way to become an expert is to publish your own book.

As you look around our society, experts have books. They're the people we look to when we need counsel or advice.

They're whom we go to when we have a problem or need a solution (like I did when I knew a change was coming). That's why it's so important for local business owners to position themselves as experts. Being recognized as <u>the most credible source</u> of information in your industry is, by far, the best way to dominate your market and grow your business. And when you put the word "Author" after your name, you most definitely command attention.

Most business owners fight for the attention of the public through traditional media and online venues. These are all important and valuable, but they are also very crowded and make differentiating yourself difficult. When you hand someone a copy of your book, you immediately step outside the traditional battle ground and establish yourself as someone who has something to say… and who should be listened to. This makes all the difference in the world.

Winning the Battle

In their legendary book, *Positioning*, marketing experts and authors Al Ries and Jack Trout tell us that:

<u>**Marketing is a battle for position in the mind of the customer**</u>.

Handing your prospect a copy of your book (especially a personally signed copy) immediately puts you in a more favorable position.

Until now publishing a book was out of reach for most small business owners. Large publishers want nothing to do with you, and even if they did show some interest, you'd still have to labor for hours and days and months writing your book and getting it into a form that you could submit to them, only to be rejected time after time.

Or you could go the self-publishing route that has become more popular recently. The problem with this route is that you still have to spend hours and days and weeks laboring in front of your computer typing away night after night, day after day. Who has time for that? Then, once you have your thoughts out of your head, now you have to go through dozens of pages to edit, proofread, add pictures, think about a title, create a cover, and secure an ISBN number along with a dozen other little details. And you still need to find someone to publish your book. And if you have issues or questions during this process, you have the privilege of asking friends, searching online or reading a forum looking for an answer. And if you do choose to use an online publisher, instead of talking with someone in person, most times you are required to submit a "help desk ticket" hoping someone will get back with you in 24-48 hours. Ever been there???

After I went through this entire process to publish my own book—*On Marketing: The Definitive Guide for Small Business Owners*—(you can get a free copy of my book by downloading the Expert Publishing Guide at www.90DayAuthor.com) I finally understood why more business owners don't publish their own book. Who has time for all of this? And the process can be a nightmare!

One day as I was spending some time in prayer seeking a way to grow my business and help local business owners grow their companies, the Lord gave me the idea to help business owners bridge the gap between having an idea for a book and actually getting one published. That idea has now become 90Day Author.

Simplifying the Process

I took that idea and transformed it into a business with its own proprietary process that removes all of the hurdles to publishing your book, yet allows you to retain full control and all of the profits. We designed the website (www.90DayAuthor.com), created the process, wrote the documents, ordered business cards, and implemented our marketing plan. What a blur of activity!

As the dust settled, what appeared was a process where we work with you to outline your book and design it from cover to cover. We then employ our *Speak to Write* system to capture your book in audio form. From here we transcribe, proofread and edit your book until it's in final form. You are involved throughout the process, but we are doing most of the heavy lifting. In 90 days you'll be holding your own paperback book in your hands, and reading your book on your Kindle®.

This is where we move into the Promote stage of our process and provide you with proven marketing strategies to attract new customers, retain existing customers, and stimulate referrals like never before. And we back it up with a **1 Year Risk Free Money Back Guarantee** (get the details when you download our Free Expert Publishing Guide at www.90DayAuthor.com or by scanning this QR code).

Becoming an author is one of the most rewarding (and profitable) marketing strategies available to you. You've probably thought about writing a book at some point in your life. Now you can. Learn how you can become a 90Day Author by downloading our Free Expert Publishing Guide: www.90DayAuthor.com.

Getting Started

Once I had everything in place, it was time to embark on my own marketing strategy. I decided to begin with the basics–getting face-to-face meetings.

I knew that I needed to meet some business owners and others who know business owners. As I was considering my options (there are many places where business people gather), I decided to visit a few BNI® (Business Networking International) groups. After visiting 5 groups in 3 weeks, I realized that this was a great organization and most definitely the right place for me.

Within three weeks, I had met with a number of people, and four of them chose to begin the process of becoming a 90Day Author. Since that time, we continue to see rapid growth as we help business owners tell their story in a new and exciting way. We are managing the growth and expanding our team to ensure that we continually provide superior customer service and an excellent product (I learned the importance of having reliable systems from my co-authors Roger Best and Mike Davidson). We take what we do very seriously because as a 90Day Author, your name is on the line—and so is ours.

In addition to 90Day Author, I also operate a marketing strategy firm with a few private clients. To help you more fully understand how I think about marketing, I've included a few marketing tips and strategies in the following pages. These strategies can be used by anyone in business. However, I believe that being an author is one of the best marketing strategies available to you, whether you are an owner, partner or salesperson.

As a businessperson, you are constantly marketing yourself and your business. You should always be searching for new ways to position yourself in a "category of one" so that you become <u>the obvious choice</u> for those needing your help. There are a variety of methods you can use to accomplish this. However, the most productive (and cost effective) method is to become a 90Day Author.

You can learn more about our process and how becoming a 90Day Author can help you grow your business when you **download our FREE Expert Publishing Guide** from our website www.90DayAuthor.com or by scanning this QR code.

I look forward to serving you and seeing your name on the cover of *your* own book!

To Your Growth,

Michael W. DeLon
Author & Founder | 90Day Author

Marketing Strategies To Grow Your Business

7 SMART Ideas

I like to work smart. And I like my marketing to be SMART. SMART is an acronym I use for:

Strategic
Measurable
Automated
Response-Oriented
Tactical

If your marketing isn't SMART then you are wasting a lot of your hard earned money. The strategies you'll learn here will help you create a SMART Marketing Plan for your business. Underlying everything I do are these fundamental ideas. For our purposes here, we'll call them:

The 7 SMART Ideas:

1. Marketing is a Battle of Positioning that's fought in the Mind of the Customer.

>You want to be the 1st person people think of when your product category is mentioned.

2. Choose Your Customer Wisely

>You don't need to sell to everybody. In fact, that's a recipe for failure. The more selective you can be, the more growth you will experience.

3. Position Yourself Purposefully

> You have to stand for something or you will fall for anything. What is it that makes you different? How will you stand out from the crowd? Your positioning is critical.

4. Words are the Greatest Creative Force

> When God created the world He spoke it into existence. For you to create massive business growth, you too will need to use words. Images and Logos are helpful, but words are what cause people to take action.

5. Know What Your Customer is Actually Paying For

> People don't care about you or your product. They care about themselves and what your product can do for them. Speak to their needs and your business will grow.

6. Marketing is a Process, Not an Event

> Sporadic marketing is a waste of time and money. You need a plan if you're going to grow your business and achieve your dreams and goals. The more consistent you are in your marketing, the greater growth you will experience.
>
> Marketing effects take place over time. Plan to be patient and consistent.

7. You Are In the Attraction Business

>I don't know what business you *think* you are in, but you are really in the Attraction Business. The day you stop attracting new customers is the day your business begins to die.

The Key to Market Domination

Nike. Coca-Cola. FedEx. Apple. Amazon. eBay. Geico.

The list could go on and on. Leaders one and all. But HOW did they get to the top? What caused them to break through the clutter, claim the #1 spot, and stay there?

In a word: *Positioning*.

To be successful—to DOMINATE your market—you have to be in touch with reality. And in marketing, the only reality is in the mind of your customer.

Marketing is a battle of positioning that's fought in the mind of the customer.

It's not important whether or not you have a better product or service or reputation or warranty. What matters is *HOW* you are positioned in the mind of your customer.

In every customer's head, for every product category, there is a ladder. On each rung of that ladder, there is a company. **Your objective is to occupy the top rung of your product category in the mind of your customer.** That way, whenever your product category is mentioned, customers immediately think of YOU!

YOU become the default.
YOU become their go-to source.
YOU become their first and only choice.

THIS is the Position YOU must plan to have.

Remember: the fastest and easiest way for you to gain this type of positioning is to become a 90Day Author.

The 3 Stages of Business

Every business is comprised of the same 3 Stages. Whether you are a mom & pop operation or a multi-national conglomerate, at the end of the day all businesses have these same three stages.

The 3 Stages of Business are:

Attract | Engage | Retain

```
         Attract
         /    \
    Engage ←→ Retain
```

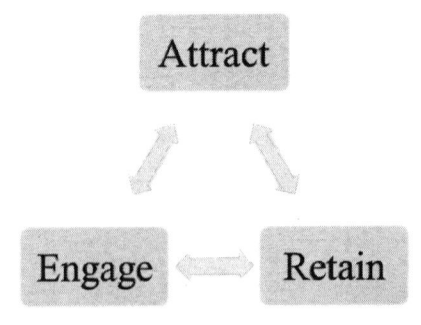

The ATTRACT Stage is where you are attracting prospects and customers TO your business. It encompasses everything from how you are perceived in the marketplace by the customer (think positioning), to your reputation, the message you deliver, and the offers you make. It also includes the visual aspects of your business like your logo design (as Mike Bennett discussed in his chapter) as well as the look of your building and the parking area and lighting. All of these and a lot more are part of your Attract Stage. It's everything you are doing to Attract new customers TO your business.

In the Attract Stage you want to consider what it is that your customer is actually buying from you. Too many times business owners only sell features, or worse yet, they sell by price. You don't want to play that game. Give your customers what they want.

Every year millions of quarter inch drill bits are manufactured and sold. Would you believe that not one person who purchased a drill bit actually wanted to own one?

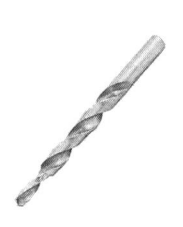

The drill bit manufacturer tells everyone about the quality of their drill bit, the type of steel they use to make their drill bit, and the employees who make the drill bit.

All of this falls into the category of "Who cares?"

The customer does not want a drill bit.

The customer wants…a hole!

www.BigBusinessInLittleRock.com

Speak to what it is that your customer is actually paying for and you'll Attract a lot more customers and make a lot more sales.

So now that you have attracted a customer, we move into the **ENGAGE Stage**. This is where your customer begins to connect with you in some way.

It could be that they hear or see your message and go to your website. They might call you. They could even walk through your front door. However they connect with you, that is when the Attract Stage ends and the Engage Stage begins.

NOTE: You must make certain that what you tell them in the Attract Stage matches, or is exceeded by, what they experience in the Engage Stage. Otherwise you'll deliver a bad customer experience and you'll run them away...and they'll take their friends with them.

Haven't we all had the experience of hearing about a new restaurant in town (no offense to restaurant owners)? They talk about how great the food is and their wonderful service. So you go there for dinner only to experience a noisy atmosphere, small portions of adequate food and servers who are too busy doing other things to care for your needs. How likely are you to return?

How likely are you to tell your friends to go there? That's what happens when your Attract and Engage Stages are not in sync.

The Engage Stage is a hidden gold mine that many business owners overlook. Don't make that mistake. You need to look carefully at how you Engage with your customers and make certain you are giving them what they really want.

Forget about the drill bit. Focus on the hole!

Now we come to the **Retain Stage**. This is where most business owners fail. And that's unfortunate because the Retain Stage is where wealth is created in a business. It's where you Retain *Customers for Life* and gain their Repeat & Referral business.

The Retain Stage is where you are building an on-going relationship with your customer. You are not only sending them "Thank You" notes for their purchase, you are calling them, sending them newsletters, inviting them to special events and giving them special offers and exclusive benefits.

You make them feel special—because they are special. They are your customers! They have purchased your product or service. Don't ever allow them to feel like an unloved or an un-cared-for orphan.

The Retain Stage can become one of the most profitable stages in your business. The likeliest type of customer to get to purchase from you again is a satisfied customer. It takes 7-10 times more money to Attract a new customer than it does to Retain an existing customer.

The Retain Stage is the *least* expensive portion of your marketing mix. It's the one where you can have the biggest impact with the least amount of money, because they already know you. That's really what you're doing, isn't it? You're making sure that when they have a need, they are going to think of you first, and more often than not, they are going to use you again... and not be tempted to try someone else just because they're being offered a lower price. You must stay in contact with them. Repeat business is just the tip of the iceberg in growing your business.

To grow your business quickly, invest some focused effort on your Retain Stage and you'll begin seeing your profits go straight to the bottom line.

The Alphabet Maze

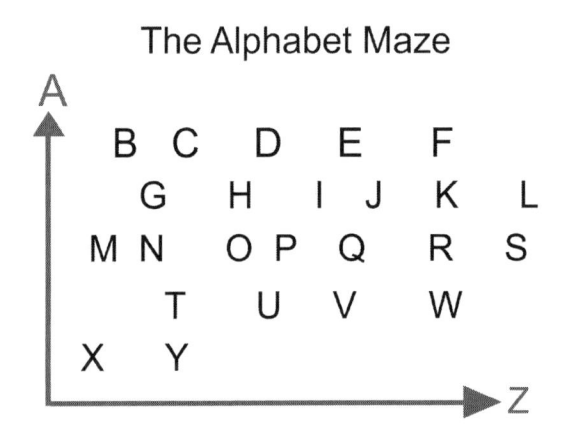

```
              The Alphabet Maze
     A
     ↑    B   C   D   E   F
          G   H   I   J   K   L
        M N   O   P   Q   R   S
              T   U   V   W
          X   Y
     └─────────────────────→ Z
```

The path that your customer takes on their way to a purchase is what I refer to as The Alphabet Maze.

Every customer has a slightly different path they will take. Some will move fast while others meander. Whatever their pace, it is YOUR RESPONSIBILITY to lead them through this Maze so that they end up at their desired destination.

Most business people want to take someone from A to Z as quickly as possible. And if the customer "just isn't ready to make a decision today", then the salesperson leaves them and looks for someone else to help.

That's very short sighted! Always remember that:

Between A and Z there's a great big B through Y.

A better tactic is to **establish a process** that allows people to come through The Alphabet Maze at their own pace. You will be guiding them the entire way, giving them information, answering their questions, building trust and becoming their advocate. This way, WHEN THEY ARE READY to make a purchase, YOU are their only logical choice.

To lead them through this Maze takes some forethought on your part. It can consist of a series of Free Reports or Pre-Written Emails that you have set up in an Auto-Responder to go out on a predetermined time frame, your Free Recorded Message, or even invite them to a special VIP event.

At this stage you are wooing then, building trust, and establishing yourself as THE SOURCE and THE SOLUTION to their needs (being a 90Day Author <u>really</u> helps you here).

YOU are the expert. YOU have what they need. It is up to YOU to win their heart, overcome their concerns, remove any and every barrier to inaction (more on this later) and assure them – then re-assure them – that they will be completely taken care of and have no risk doing business with you.

The Alphabet Maze is an extremely powerful concept that helps you build trust with your prospects so that they become not only clients, but customers for life.

The Marketing Triad

Any stool worth its weight has only 3 legs. Any fewer and it will topple; any more and it will rock. Three is the perfect number.

Similarly, your marketing should be founded on three as well. I call these 3 components **The Marketing Triad**.

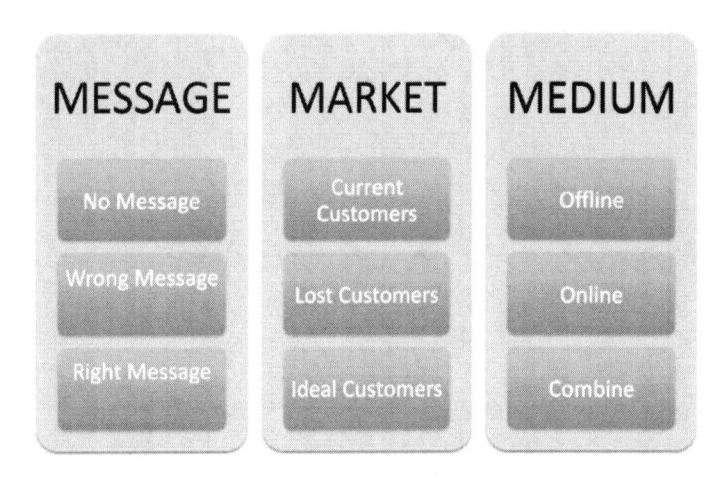

MESSAGE	MARKET	MEDIUM
No Message	Current Customers	Offline
Wrong Message	Lost Customers	Online
Right Message	Ideal Customers	Combine

The three components of every marketing strategy and campaign are your Message, Market and Medium.

Too often a business person completely ignores the Message, never chooses a specific target Market, and picks a Medium either by random selection, most often because they've always used this one, or due to the presence of a media rep standing in their doorway reminding them of a deadline that's fast approaching. None of these are the right way to market.

To grow your business you need to understand and use the three parts of The Marketing Triad.

MESSAGE

Your MESSAGE is critical. It is the foundation for your Position in the Market (which you'll remember is found in the mind of the customer).

Seldom do you find a local business with a strong, compelling, benefit oriented Message that they deliver consistently to a specific group of people.

Most businesses have No Message at all. Their marketing is nothing more than Name, Rank and Serial Number. Price is the only thing they have to offer. This is a BAD Message. What this tells the customer is that you have nothing else to offer. You *are* just like everyone else (just as they suspected) and there's **no reason** for them to choose to do business with you.

When you have No Message, you have a very strong message in the wrong direction.

Other businesses have the Wrong Message. They talk about how great they are as a company, how long they've been in business, the lines of product they carry, and their wonderful staff that has a combined experience of 1,000 years.

All of this falls into the category of what??? That's right:

Who Cares???!!!!

Customers don't buy your products for the features. They buy for the benefits they will receive from owning.

Speak in terms of what owning your product/service will do for them. Paint a picture that they'll not only remember, but also desire. I call it "future pacing." It's allowing them to envision what life will be like when they own your product/service, and how great everything will be.

Saying the right thing is the first part of developing your positioning and differentiating yourself in the marketplace. And it's the second most important part of creating a marketing strategy that results in rapid customer attraction and sustainable business growth.

MARKET

The most important component in developing your marketing plan is to say the right message *to* the right market.

We call this the Message to Market Match.

The reason this is THE MOST IMPORTANT is that you can say the Right Thing to the WRONG person and your results are going to be less than you desire. Simply blasting it out through traditional media channels (radio, newspaper, outdoor, magazines, cable/tv, etc.) is precisely what you are doing.

Will you get some response doing this? Yes. Would you get a better response by carefully choosing a target market that is "hungry" for what you offer? Absolutely. Is this much more difficult to do? Not at all. In fact, it's simple, once you know how to do it.

The Market component of The Marketing Triad breaks your "market" down into 3 buckets:

Current Customers, Lost Customers & Ideal Customers

These types of customers are just the start, but when you focus on these three, you'll find that you'll get a much faster (and larger) ROI on your marketing efforts.

Current customers are your best source for increased income. They already Know, Like & Trust you. Your job is to give them even more reasons to buy more from you and offer them other buying options that they'd never expect you to offer.

There's an entire process called Joint Venture Marketing that we don't have time for here, but suffice it to say, that when you learn how to structure and execute a Joint Venture that adds value for your current customers, your profits will increase and your customer retention will be much higher. If you're interested in learning a bit about Joint Venture Marketing and how it can help you increase your profits (or in joining one of our Catalyst Business Growth Groups), let me know by emailing me from my website: www.90DayAuthor.com.

Lost customers pose another great opportunity for business growth. That's because there are only about <u>6 reasons people stop doing business with you</u>, and many of those can be overcome.

Here are the top reasons people stop doing business with you:

68% upset with the treatment they've received
14% dissatisfied with product or service
9% begin doing business with a competitor
5% seek alternatives or develop other business relationships
3% move away
1% die

96% of your Lost Customers are still buying what you sell. They're just buying it from someone else.

Now we move on to Ideal Customers. This is where the BIG MONEY is! You need to know a couple of things if you're going to grow your business:

What is the Lifetime Value of Your Customer?
Who is Your Ideal Customer?

The answers to these two questions will help you target your Message to the Right Market more rapidly.

Knowing the Lifetime Value (LTV) of a Customer is a critical number because it affects how you look at every part of your business and marketing. Here's a simple way to calculate this number for your business:

Average Amount of a Purchase $ _____
Average # of Purchases / yr   _____
Average # of years you serve a customer _____

Multiply these numbers together and you'll have the Lifetime Value of your Average Customer. For Example:

$150 Average Purchase
X   3 Purchases per year
X   8 Years of purchasing

= $3,600 as the Lifetime Value of a Customer.

Now you know that every new customer you attract is worth NOT $150 (the initial sale), but $3,600 (their LTV). *THAT* will change the way you treat him or her from the very start!

Determine WHO your Ideal Customer is, know their Lifetime Value, and use this information to make better decisions that will put more money in your bank each and every month.

So we've talked about the importance of your Message. You now understand the different components of your Market. The final part of The Marketing Triad is the Medium that you will use.

MEDIUM

At its very basic level, the Medium is the Delivery Method. It's the vehicle that you will use to get your Message to your Market. At the ground level, there is OFFLINE Media and ONLINE Media.

OFFLINE is what we refer to as "traditional" media: Newspaper, Radio, Outdoor, Direct Mail, Magazines, TV, Cable, etc.

ONLINE encompasses: Websites, Email, Blogs, Social Media Platforms, Podcast, Videos, etc.

A very common approach is to chase the New at the expense of the Old. Business owners far and wide are hypnotized by the next new "shiny object" that appears as their Prince Charming who's going to ride into town and save them from all of their idiotic marketing mishaps.

They hear about the newest whatever and spend time, energy and money chasing it, dabbling in it, and getting distracted by it. All the while their business is falling off because they are no longer giving any attention to the one who "brought them to the dance."

Hear me now: I'm all in favor of online media. And I am passionate about offline media. A better approach is to bring them together in what I call, **COMBINE Media**.

The more you can use multiple platforms to convey your Message to your Market using a variety of Media, the better results you will get.

However—and this is A BIG HOWEVER, you need to fully understand this principle of marketing:

NEVER

buy a bigger media provider

than you can afford to be a BIG PLAYER on.

As Marketing Consultant and Author Roy Williams says,

"There is No Future Being a Small Fish in a Big Pond."

It is much more productive, not to mention more profitable, to be a Big Fish in a Small Pond. That way everyone knows who you are. And when they know who you are, they're more likely to do business with you (here's another place where being an author can help you).

Now you know the importance of crafting the Right Message, targeting the Right Market and using the Right Medium so that your own Marketing Triad will produce measureable results.

The 1 Question You Must Answer

So much money is wasted in marketing every day because people don't answer this one simple question.

It's not a difficult question at all. The challenge exists because we are not taught to anticipate this question—therefore, we do not answer this question.

This one question is THE question that every customer is asking himself or herself before taking a step in your direction (think Alphabet Maze) and before they ever buy from you (think Removing the Barriers to Inaction). It's a question that you must answer convincingly and repeatedly.

The question that every customer is asking that you must answer is simply:

What's In It For Me?

That's really all the customer wants to know. But instead of telling them what's in it for them, most business owners drone on and on about how great they are (remember the drill bit and the hole????). As a business owner:

YOU ARE *INSIDE* THE BOTTLE
      LOOKING OUT
TRYING TO SEE YOURSELF.

It's extremely difficult for you to "see" what your customer sees. That's why it's important to gain the perspective of others who have the expertise to tell you there's a rip in your sail or a hole in your boat.

Your customer is far too busy to be concerned about you. They are only interested in what your product/service can do for them, and how it can satisfy some of their deepest longings. Sometimes these longings are needs; sometimes they are desires. Regardless of what they are, if you don't effectively answer this one question, you will lose more sales than you make.

Fulcrum Positioning

Integrating Strategies for Greater Growth

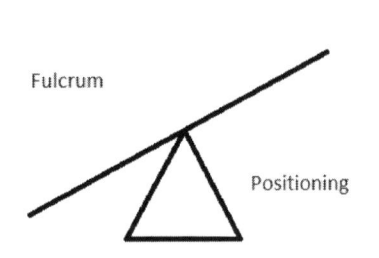

A fulcrum is the point on which a lever rests or is supported and on which it pivots. In this image, it's where the top of the triangle touches the lever.

To gain greater leverage in your marketing, which leads to greater growth and more profits, you need to develop methods to reposition the fulcrum so that you can have greater output for the same amount of input.

The simplest fulcrum is a teeter-totter. The fulcrum is in the middle so that the input force exerted on one-end equals the output force on the other. Because it's a balanced system, it will give you a 1:1 ratio. That's why a smaller child has to sit farther back when teetering with a heavier child.

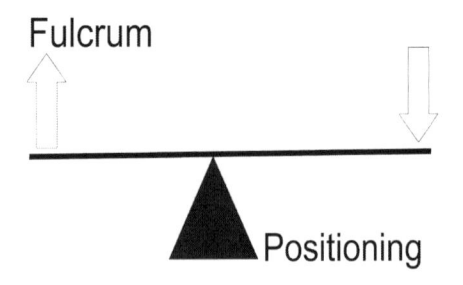

Another way to manipulate this situation is to move the fulcrum (not as easy to do with teeter-totters as it is with your marketing). By relocating the fulcrum, you gain an advantage through the creation of a lever.

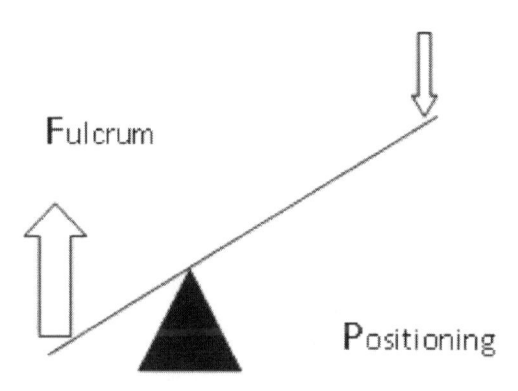

And with careful positioning of your fulcrum, and the right lever, you can create a multiplying effect from your marketing. When you do this properly, you end up putting IN the same amount of time, energy, money and resources, but you are getting OUT much more in sales, profits and income.

Brochures, Business Cards & Other Throwaways

I'm not a huge fan of dog tags. I know they serve their purpose, but beyond that they can be pretty useless. The "dog tags" I'm referring to are not the kind used to identify military personnel. I'm referring to those identifiers that we all "wear" to communicate what we do.

Almost everyone has a business card. Heavens, even my 14 year-old son has a business card for his lawn mowing business. And come to think about it, he has a brochure as well. Now his are a bit different than most, but still, he has them.

Most business cards contain name, rank and serial number. They are basic, banal, and blah. Their primary use is as a memory aid while talking to someone new so that you can remember their name until your conversation is over.

And brochures are some of the biggest waste of paper on earth. Do you really think that people are that interested in your company and products? Remember: They are only interested in *WIIFM?* and more often than not, your brochure isn't answering that question.

So what are you to do, throw these all away? No, don't do that. Instead, you should repurpose them so that they communicate in a way that's engaging and memorable. You can use your business card as a lead-in to your 24/7 Free Recorded Message or to download your Free Report at your website. <u>Your business card should be mostly about your prospect and secondarily about you.</u>

Why are you in business anyway? Isn't it to serve others? What better way to serve your future customers than by giving them a business card that will move them a step closer to actually doing business with you!

It may take a bit of thought on your part—and it will definitely take some courage—but when you hand someone your business card and it gives them an immediate benefit, not only will it begin to position you as different, it will cause them to know, like and trust you more. That is a great thing!

This is one of my business cards...

Michael W. DeLon - Publisher   **Prepare   Produce   Publish   Promote**

📖90Day Author

Publish Your Book in 90 Days Without Writing a Sentence

Free Book: **10 Ways To Build Your Business By Publishing A Book** at 90DayAuthor.com

---

Notice how it doesn't say much about me?! It's focused purposefully <u>on my prospect</u> and "What's In It For *Them*." I even offer them a FREE book from my website.

No phone number. No address. No email. They can find all of those at my website; and believe me, they do!

The beauty of this card is that is begs the question, "How do you do that?"

That's *exactly* the question I want them to ask because now we're in a conversation about the uniqueness of what I offer and how they can benefit from becoming a 90Day Author.

So take a look at your business card and brochures. Try to see them through your prospect's eyes. *What's In It For Them*? Consider these questions:

> > What is it that you are communicating?
> > Why should they care?
> > What are you offering to do for them?
> > How can you help them?

These are the questions you need to be asking yourself (and your staff) on a regular basis. <u>Stay focused on your customer</u> and your business will grow.

---

www.BigBusinessInLittleRock.com

Putting It All Together

You now have the basic building blocks for a solid foundation upon which to construct your own marketing program. You've been given the strategies, concepts and tactics to build your business. And you have the blueprint formula to view your business in its Three Stages.

Now it's time for you to go to work.

If you haven't done so already, analyze your business in regards to The Three Stages of Business. Consider how you want to bring your customers through The Alphabet Maze, and work on your Message, Market and Medium choices.

This is where most people fall off. They read a chapter like this and say, "I'll get to that tomorrow" and then put the book on their desk. A few weeks later they find it under a stack of papers, briefly flip through it, then put it on the shelf with a dozen or more other "good intention" books that they've read.

Your business won't change until <u>you</u> do something to change it.

You have to take <u>action</u>. You have to take what you've learned here—even if it's just one idea, concept or strategy—and **apply it** to your business.

I learned these phrases early in my sales career and they have served me well ever since:

>Education Without Action Is Entertainment.

>To Know And Not To Do Is Not To Know.

My time management philosophy is: **Do It Now!**

If you lack motivation, take a few moments to visualize the future you desire. What will it be like when you are Attracting customers on autopilot, Engaging with them profitably, and Retaining them for Life? How will your life change when your sales, profits and income are continually rising, even in "bad economic times"? What is it that you really want your life to be like?

It's possible! But it requires discipline, focus and <u>action</u>. As you begin to create the marketing for your business, don't worry about getting it perfect. It doesn't need to be.

Get it done and get it out.

Begin a 30-Day Challenge by setting some realistic yet challenging goals that you can go after in the next month. Don't bite off more than you can chew, but be aggressive. You'll be surprised at how much you can accomplish when you have a dream, make a plan, and decide to let nothing stand in your way.

I hope that our paths cross someday so I can hear what you accomplished by implementing the strategies you learned from reading this chapter. Who knows, perhaps you'll become a 90Day Author or be featured in the next edition of *Big Business in Little Rock*.

What I Like About Little Rock

When we moved here in 2004 to serve with the ministry of FamilyLife, we knew that we'd found a great place to live. Our family has enjoyed climbing Pinnacle Mountain, biking on the many trails in the area, and the beauty of the outdoors.

The business climate here is exciting. The "Southern hospitality" extends to business relationships as a natural way of connecting with one another. Conversations are easy, and common ground is quickly found. There are ample "hometown" restaurants and wonderful locally owned coffee shops scattered throughout many neighborhoods which are great for business meetings, or for the many dates I've had with my sons and wife.

The other thing I really enjoy about Little Rock is the convenience. You can get almost anywhere in 20 minutes. What a blessing this is when you consider many people spend 45–90 minutes in their car every day driving to and from work. What a joy to have everything you need within a few minutes! It's also nice to have an airport that's not only easy and fast to get to, but that is small enough to navigate quickly.

When I started my company, I could have easily moved my family back to Indiana, or anywhere else for that matter. But we chose to stay in Little Rock. As we've asked ourselves the question, "Where else would we like to live?", we keep coming back to the same answer. Little Rock is now "home" for the DeLon family and will be until the Lord moves us on.

All in all, Little Rock is a great place to live and to do business. It's no wonder there are so many small businesses finding big success in this "little" city.

2 Special Offers

1. FREE 1-Hour Marketing Audit

Whether you choose to become a 90Day Author or not, you'll benefit greatly from having a fresh set of eyes looking into your business. You'll walk away with new perspectives and actionable strategies you can implement immediately. Regardless of the size or type of business you may have, this 1-Hour Marketing Audit will add value to your company in the coming year.

Most business owners approach marketing like a roulette wheel; like a game of chance. Through this 1-Hour Marketing Audit, you'll learn how to <u>step away from the roulette wheel and aim for the marketing bull's eye</u>.

Request Your Complimentary 1-Hour Marketing Audit Today:

1-877-850-2505

2. Complimentary 90Day Author Assessment

This is a service we provide to help you discern if publishing a book can help you grow your business. This complimentary 30-minute Author Interview will help you more fully understand our process, review your book ideas and consider possible marketing strategies and timelines.

Request Your Complimentary 90Day Author Assessment:

1-877-850-2505

www.BigBusinessInLittleRock.com

About Michael

Michael DeLon is the founder of 90Day Author. He's an author, marketing strategist and business growth coach who specializes in helping small business people position themselves as "the expert" by publishing their own book. Then Michael teaches them how to use their book to Attract, Engage and Retain customers for life while stimulating Referrals.

He's a straight shooter with over 25 years of experience studying, applying, and fine-tuning these marketing strategies, which allows him to find SMART Solutions that others never see.

Marketing doesn't have to be a gamble. Michael can help you step away from the Advertising Roulette Wheel and Aim for the Marketing Bull's Eye. He can also help you become a recognized Expert by helping you publish your own book!

Michael is the husband of one and father of three. He's a committed follower of Jesus Christ and is deeply involved in his church. You can normally find Michael investing time with his family or helping others grow their marketing and their marriage relationship.

You can contact Michael through his website:

<u>www.90DayAuthor.com</u>

Conclusion

We hope you have enjoyed this "peek behind the curtain" into our lives and the businesses that we operate. Our desire is that these few pages have helped you to remember, or discover for the first time, why Little Rock is a great place to live and do business.

We all need to do our part to make Little Rock an even better city. Look around at what YOU can do to invest in the lives of others, make a difference for a non-profit and support a locally owned and operated small business. As you do this, we'll all benefit and you'll find great satisfaction in knowing that you are helping to create another Big Business in Little Rock.

Thanks for reading *Big Business in Little Rock*. We look forward to serving you.

Contact Us

Roger Best
BizTek Connection
Phone: 866-851-5321
Web: www.BizTekConnection.com

Jason Everett
Liberty National Insurance
Phone: (501) 225-5556
Web: www.libertynational-everett.com/

Mike Davidson
Parkway Automotive
Phone: (501) 821-6111
Web: www.ParkwayAutomotive.net

J. Ted Lewis
Floral Express Flower Market
Phone: (800) 7362841
Web: www.floralx.com

Mike Bennett
Bennett Design Group / Sir Speedy
Phone: (501) 221-0200
Web: www.sirspeedy.com/centers/littlerockar020/
       www.bdglr.com

Michael W. DeLon
90Day Author
Phone: (877) 850-2505
Web: www.90DayAuthor.com